SPACINGS

of Reason and Imagination

SPAC

JOHN SALLIS

N G S—

of Reason and Imagination

IN TEXTS OF

Kant, Fichte, Hegel

THE UNIVERSITY OF CHICAGO PRESS

Chicago and London

JOHN SALLIS is Arthur J. Schmitt Professor of
Philosophy at Loyola University of Chicago. Among
his many books are *Delimitations: Phenomenology and
the End of Metaphysics, The Gathering of Reason,* and
Being and Logos: The Way of Platonic Dialogue. He is
the editor of *Deconstruction and Philosophy: The Texts of
Jacques Derrida,* also published by the University of
Chicago Press.

The University of Chicago Press, Chicago 60637
The University of Chicago Press, Ltd., London

© 1987 by The University of Chicago
All rights reserved. Published 1987
Printed in the United States of America

96 95 94 93 92 91 90 89 88 87   5 4 3 2 1

Library of Congress Cataloging-in-Publication Data

Sallis, John, 1938–
    Spacings of reason and imagination in texts
of Kant, Fichte, Hegel.
    Includes index.
    1. Kant, Immanuel, 1724–1804. 2. Fichte,
Johann Gottlieb, 1762–1814. 3. Hegel, Georg
Wilhelm Friedrich, 1770–1831. 4. Reason—History.
5. Imagination (Philosophy)—History. I. Title.
B2743.S35   1987   141'.0943   86-11417
ISBN 0-226-73440-4
ISBN 0-226-73441-2 (pbk.)

CONTENTS

ACKNOWLEDGMENTS

I would like to express my gratitude to the American Council of Learned Societies for the fellowship that allowed me to devote myself to the present project during the 1982–83 academic year.

I am grateful also to the staff of the Hegel-Archiv of the Ruhr-Universität Bochum, especially to Hans-Christian Lucas, who made available to me the unpublished transcriptions of Hegel's lectures done by Hotho and by Griesheim, and to Friedrich Hogemann, who was most generous in deciphering for me the difficult script of these transcriptions. I would like also to thank the Staatsbibliothek Preussischer Kulturbesitz, Berlin, for permission to cite from these transcriptions.

"Tunnelings"—in an earlier draft—was first presented at a conference organized at the State University of New York at Stony Brook by Hugh Silverman, whom I wish to thank for that occasion. It was also the subject of valuable discussions with David Krell in St. Ulrich. A portion of "Enroutings" is based on a paper entitled "The Common Root," which I prepared for the Fifth International Kant Congress in Mainz. "Ending(s)" is an expanded version of a paper "Imagination and Presentation in Hegel's Philosophy of Spirit," which I presented at the 1984 meetings of the Hegel Society of America.

Special thanks to Jill Lavelle and to Lauren and Jerry.

J. S.

OCCLUSION

a | Spacing—reiterated lapse, almost without limit; slippage into the open, spreading truth even into untruth, separating it from itself in a way that would once have been called separation *as such,* the advent of crisis, a crisis of truth, of reason. It is also the condition for a preface, the lodging of the preface.

And yet, after Hegel it is not only a question of the preface, assuming that one could indeed ever write, ever prove to have written, anything else. After Hegel one would write differently, spacing the writing with a certain difference—letting it be spaced by the spreading of truth, by crisis. Hence a critical writing, as in the following text by Nietzsche, which, punctuated exactly as it is here, he included in that chapter of *Twilight of the Idols* entitled "'Reason' in Philosophy":[1]

. . . "Reason" is the cause of our falsification of the testimony of the senses. Insofar as the senses show becoming, passing away, change, they do not lie . . . But Heraclitus will remain eternally right, that being is an empty fiction. The "apparent" world is the only one: the "true world" is merely added by a lie. . .

The spacing of this text is manifold and complex, some moments marked, others left unmarked.

Let me indicate briefly just a few points at which this textual spacing is in play, following primarily the three ellipses. The first ellipsis marks a separation between "reason" and what has immediately preceded it, namely, an enumeration of certain lies: the lie of unity, that of thinghood, and that of permanence. Nietzsche has just written also of how these lies get introduced, and he is about to accuse reason of falsifying the testimony of the senses by introducing them. But the separation of "reason" from "lies" is required, even if only to be denied in the next moment, because a reason that would propound lies, that would tell only lies about the entire world, would simply—that is, without spacing—not be reason. In a classical formulation—also itself violated and in need here of spacing—it belongs to the very sense of "reason" that it be oriented simply to truth, that it tell only the truth, not lies, about the world. Lying reason would not be reason at all, and, accordingly, in Nietzsche's text "reason" is not only separated by the ellipsis from those lies that in another moment it will be accused of telling but also separated from itself, placed in quotation marks. The opposition between lying "reason" and reason as essentially oriented to truth is spread out, the terms set apart, the difference left open.

The text continues: "Insofar as the senses show becoming, passing away, change, they do not lie." Again an opposition is broached, now an opposition not only to the determination of reason but to metaphysics as such, to metaphysical determination and to the determination of metaphysics. Not only could the assertion that the senses do not lie never be a metaphysical determination, a metaphysical assertion, something simply sayable in metaphysics; but also, especially considering that respect in which they are explicitly said not to lie (insofar as they show becoming, passing away, change), the assertion runs counter to the very sense—here again spacing is required—of metaphysical determination as such, that the sense of something is not its appearance to the senses, that a certain turn from the senses to truth is necessary. The assertion is opposed to this turn, to metaphysics as such; the separation is marked not only by the second ellipsis—reading it as marking the omission of metaphysics—but also by what follows that ellipsis, by the invocation of a premetaphysical thinker, in fact, the one whom Nietzsche regarded as most decisively countermetaphysical, even though, as Nietzsche also indicates in this context,

"Heraclitus too did the senses an injustice." But in the regard that is decisive here "Heraclitus will remain eternally right, that being is an empty fiction." How would it be possible ever to have been more decisively countermetaphysical: not only is being declared a lie (being—that is, the truth to which metaphysical reason turns), but that very declaration is declared eternally right, that is, eternally true—that is, its very declaration must be kept separated from what is declared, a spacing operative between them, marked here by the name "Heraclitus."

Thus, it is declared that the "apparent" world is the only one, that the "true world" is merely added by a lie (*ist nur hinzugelogen*). The story of that addition, the history of metaphysics, the story of how the "true world" finally became a fable—this story is about to be told. Thus, a certain genealogical narrative will come to explicate the sense—here again, spacing—of the addition, the sense in which the "true world" is merely added by a lie. But what of the other sense of being thus declared in the declaration that the "apparent" world *is* the only one? Here there must supervene a spacing as displacement, twisting one term loose from the opposition, separating it from itself. It is of this spacing that the story tells in its final episode—marking it with an ellipsis:[2]

The true world we have abolished: what world has remained? the apparent one perhaps? . . . But no! *with the true world we have also abolished the apparent one!*

The "true world"—unless, as here, in a story—requires the spacing of the quotation marks, because it is merely a story, a fable, something told again and again, a kind of quotation. But with the "apparent" world—referring again to the initial text cited—it is quite different: in this case the spacing marked by the quotation marks is one of separation between that world *as* appearance and that world *as* . . .

The "true world," the world of unity, thinghood, permanence, is the composite lie added in such a way as to falsify the testimony of the senses, added by "reason." Thus, Nietzsche's text declares reason to be the cause of the falsification.

And yet, in the same context,[3] Nietzsche indicates that when such a fable comes to be invented it is because a certain slander against life has already come into play, that is, because a certain kind of falsification of the "apparent" world is already operative. But in that case, one would, in declaring "reason" the cause of the falsification, have inverted the causal order; and reason would, then, be only what Nietzsche calls an "imaginary cause."[4] One cannot but wonder— though Nietzsche does not raise the question—what sense imagination could have here.

"Reason" is also a "false cause" in the sense that Nietzsche will soon outline, false because it is only a mask for another cause. In the "prejudices of reason," Nietzsche writes, the constant advocate of error is language:[5]

. . . "Reason" in language: oh, what an old deceptive female she is! I am afraid we are not rid of God because we still believe in grammar . . .

Little wonder, then, that spacing sets in, that writing must be critical.

b | Critically written, the text of Nietzsche announces *occlusion,* not only through its spacing, but also through what it openly declares. Occlusion, first of all, in its etymological sense, as *occludere,* to close up—hence, occlusion as what is also called the closure of metaphysics. Then, second, occlusion in the sense used of chemical substances, as absorption—hence, occlusion as the absorption of the "true world" by the "apparent" world, occlusion consummated in the exposure of being as an empty fiction, of the "true world" as merely added by a lie. But then, third, occlusion as closure in a more specific sense, as closure of the space delimited by the opposition between the "true world" and the "apparent" world, reduction of that space to the plane of appearance. Thus, finally, occlusion as obstruction, as closing off, blocking, free passage out of or through the space (or, rather, in this case, across the plane) that remains—hence, occlusion as putting in force those oppositions that obstruct appropriation and its writing, those oppositions that broach spacing in such a way as to compel writing to be critical.

Occlusion is itself a spacing. It is that spacing that disrupts the space, the delimitation of the space, between the "true world" and the "apparent" world, that closes it off, reduces it to the plane of appearance. More precisely, it destabilizes that space, lets spaces be indefinitely inserted so as to extend it. Thus, as the story recounds,[6] the true world becomes, first, unattainable for now but promised (*"it becomes female,* it becomes Christian"); then, unattainable, indemonstrable, unpromisable, merely an imperative ("Königsbergian"); then, unattained, unknown, hence not obligating ("the first yawn of reason"—which, one might presume, will fall asleep with the coming of day); and, finally, useless and superfluous, hence refuted, hence to be abolished ("let us abolish it!"). Occlusion is, then, the spacing that sets the "true world" adrift, that lets it drift so utterly out of sight that there remains only the "apparent" world. But the latter is then displaced and becomes the scene of critical writing.

One could say, then, that occlusion is the spacing that occurs in the end of metaphysics, the final spacing of metaphysics.

Indeed, metaphysics involves spacing from the beginning, especially in the beginning, when a certain figuration produces, most notably, a line and comes thereby to delimit the space of metaphysics, not only to delimit it but also to articulate and to orient it, producing also what will later be taken as the first metaphor of metaphysics, that of ascent from a cave. Yet, however productive spacing may be in the beginning of metaphysics, still it is a spacing that would—at least retrospectively—be only provisional, no less so than the spacing of a preface. It is a spacing that would be suppressed as such, that would be stabilized as a unique space, indeed as a space that would finally prove not even to have been opened by a spacing but rather to have been always already extended, merely to be retraced. Furthermore, in being stabilized it would be rigorously distinguished from another space, a mundane space that would be enclosed (spaced) within the "apparent" world. Space would thus come to function in metaphysics only as a metaphor, a transfer between the two worlds; and spacing could only appear as a metaphoricity in which reason, oriented to the "true world" beyond, could— but ought not—get entangled. It would be a matter of utter impropriety for reason to be determined—as it will prove to be where one would perhaps least expect, in the *Critique of Pure Reason*—as tunneling, as hovering, even as ending.

The initiatory spacing is even more rigorously stabilized in modern metaphysics, the very sense of rigor being determined by that operation of stabilization. For, beginning with Descartes, but especially in the Kantian and certain "post-Kantian" texts, both that spacing and the space as which it would be stabilized and bifurcated would be drawn—that is, would prove to have been redrawn—into an interiority that, as absolute, as absolved from all exteriority, would cancel its very determination as interior, would supersede (in the sense of *Aufheben*) its own belonging to a spacing.

And yet, the text of Nietzsche announces occlusion, the final spacing of metaphysics, the spacing that releases and pluralizes spacing—spacings at the limit of metaphysics.

But what is spacing? The question is of course improper— that is, its posing requires that what is asked about in the question, namely, spacing, be already operative in it. Without spacing it cannot be asked.

But what, then, is spacing? It is a "movement" that is such as to open the very space in which it occurs. One could call it a "relation" of space to itself, a self-opening of space, providing it is distinguished sufficiently from the dialectical relation to self that would be elevated into spirit so as effectively to cancel both space and spacing. Spacing is rather a self-relation that is eccentric. Spacing always includes that obsolete sense still listed for it: to ramble, to roam.

Spacing is also an operation of typography: that of extending to a required length by inserting additional space between words, also simply that of separating words, letters, or lines by inserting space or spaces. Transitively, then, spacing is an operation of spreading something out, of inserting intervals into its interstices, of dispersing it so that it loses its compactness, its closedness. Thus, spacing leaves difference open, dis(as)sembling the plane of truth so as to set its parts at various angles to one another, reintroducing depth, a new kind of depth crossing τὸ ἀληθείας πεδίον with τὸ τῆς Λήθης πεδίον.[7]

The release of spacing opens reason beyond itself, disrupting that pure self-identity, self-recoverability, self-presence, by which spacing would be, was to have been, superseded, suppressed. It spaces reason out into a field, into various fields, for instance, those of sensibility and even of history.

Spacing is thus not simply opposed to timing, to temporalizing. For the disruption of pure self-presence, the violation of subjectivity, extends to that pure flow of interiority, pure time, that would have been, that was to have been, both distinct and yet superordinate to the exteriority identified as space. With the release of spacing there commences—or, rather, there proves always already to have commenced—a mixing of interior and exterior, an effacement of the limit, or, rather, a figuration at the limit.

Spacing is this figuration, this schematism. As such, it is (the movement of) imagination. Occlusion, the release of spacings, leads from reason to imagination.

The text that follows is stationed at the threshold of the release of spacings. That threshold is spaced out in certain Kantian and "post-Kantian" texts; I shall choose, as exemplary, certain texts of Kant, of Fichte, and of Hegel, grafting my text, as it were, onto theirs. What makes such texts the threshold of occlusion is their duplicity. On the one hand, they are the texts in which the suppression of spacing would be carried through most rigorously, the texts in which even metaphysics itself comes to be regarded as having been only an errant roaming, a spacing that must still be secured, that is to be replaced by a pure space of truth. And yet, in these very texts there occur, even if never without limits, outbreaks of spacing that would disrupt the tranquil space of reason. First, an outbreak of what can only appear as metaphoricity, reason metaphorized as tunneling; a metaphorics that serves to expose certain fissures within reason and to space reason out into its historicity. Second, a certain decentering from reason to imagination; and though a certain recentering supervenes in the end, one can— perhaps must—withdraw from that end, withdraw to imagination as the power of hovering between opposites, hence as a different spacing of truth, a spacing also beyond being. Third, the spacing of critical reason as a certain eccentricity with regard to the route that reason could follow back to the common root, that is, an eccentricity with regard to the enrouting of reason that, though categorically imperative, cannot but disrupt the very spacing of reason and broach a rout of reason. Fourth, a certain movement that would withdraw nature in its sublimity from assimilation to the supersensible space of reason, the "true world," and that would thereby draw the tremoring imagination out toward an abyss. Finally, the slightest eccentricity, traced in the very text in which imagination would be brought to its end, *aufgehoben,* within the most rigorous reduction of spacing in the entire history of metaphysics.

With all these texts, then, it is a matter of an operation at the limit, a matter of spacing.

1 | TUNNELINGS —

Reason, History, Critique

a | It is a historical irony that the Socrates of Plato's *Phaedo* turns back to his own history in such a way as to found a turning away from history that has governed the entire metaphysical tradition. In the face of death Socrates recalls how he became what he is: how he began by following the ways of his predecessors, the ways handed down through the operation of a certain tradition, the ways of that kind of wisdom called περὶ φύσεως ἱστορία; how this alleged wisdom repeatedly left him adrift; and how, finally, taking to the oars, he set out on a second voyage by having recourse to λόγοι.[1] This turn, eventually transformed into a turn from history (in the very broadest sense) to reason, remained definitive throughout the tradition, definitive *of* the tradition. It remained definitive even for the concept of tradition as such, however much this concept, mixing reason and history, submitting reason to transmission across history, continued thus to harbor the very tension that had been portrayed ironically as the Socratic turn.

The irony, however, did not remain. Instead, the turn from history to reason came eventually to be accompanied by a turn away from its own history—that is, the turn from history tended also to suppress its own history, depriving that history of any positive constitutive role. This tendency was fulfilled in those announcements of a new beginning for philosophy that introduce so many of the classic texts of seventeenth- and eighteenth- century philosophy—a new beginning to be secured by establishing philosophy once and for all beyond the futile controversies that are taken, for the most part retrospectively, to have constituted its history.

This suppression of the history of metaphysics, of the

historicity of thought, is repeated in Kant's texts. Systematic consideration of this history is consigned to that very brief final chapter of the *Critique of Pure Reason* entitled "The History of Pure Reason."[2] The title, by Kant's own testimony, merely designates an empty space in the architectonic; both the title and the few pages that it entitles do little more than mark a gap, one that must be filled out in the future (*künftig ausgefüllt werden muss*), one sufficiently inessential that its filling out can with impunity be deferred. Kant is content "with casting a cursory glance, from a purely transcendental point of view, namely, that of the nature of pure reason, on the works of those who have previously labored in this field—a glance that reveals structures, but in ruins only" (A 852/B 880). It is a matter of mere detached retrospection, of glancing back at the ruins from which the critical establishing of reason has securely detached itself.

It is little wonder that the history of metaphysics lies in ruins; from the start metaphysics got everything backward:

It is very notable, although quite naturally it could not have been otherwise, that in the infancy of philosophy men began where we should like rather to end, with the knowledge of God, occupying themselves with the hope, or rather indeed with the constitution, of another world. [A 852/B 880]

It could not have been otherwise. Why not? What is the ground of the necessity? What ground does Kant present for it? He refers to the "gross . . . religious concepts generated by the ancient practices" and traceable to "an earlier more barbarous state"; and he refers to "the more enlightened members" of society who set about to please "the invisible power that governs the world," who were thus led into "abstract inquiries of reason," into "those labors that afterward became so renowned under the name of metaphysics" (A 852–53/B 880–81). Metaphysics originated primarily from theology, and thus was destined by its very origin, its prehistory, to get everything backward from the start. And yet, wherein lies the necessity of this origin? Certainly Kant's references, a curious blend of empiricism and history, do not even begin to establish any necessity, to show that it could not have been otherwise: "Experience teaches us that a thing is so and so, but not that it cannot be otherwise" (B 3). That metaphysics necessarily got everything backward, that a reversal is necessary in order to set metaphysics on the path of science—Kant omits the demonstration, defers it, leaves it to be filled out in the future. Instead of a demonstration, Kant contents himself "with casting a cursory glance," in fact a glance that, contrary to what has been promised, decisively fails to attain "a purely transcendental point of view." He contents himself with doing little more than merely delimiting the space of that division of the system that must be filled out in the future, with merely opening the space of that division and assigning it its title, "The History of Pure Reason." What is remarkable is that he can be *content* with such a "cursory glance," despite his insistence on the *completeness* of the *Critique of Pure Reason* (cf. A xiii). One can hardly help suspecting that he can be content with deferring the history of pure reason only because the resulting empty space in the architectonic does not essentially threaten the completeness of his project. Not only does the deferral pose no threat, but also it has an essential constitutive function, which will have to be confirmed below. The virtual emptiness of that place in the system designated by the title "The History of Pure Reason" will thus prove to make explicit in the very organizing of the text a suppression of history that operates in other ways too; most important, the gap that Kant is content merely to mark will prove to reproduce at the end of the *Critique of Pure Reason,* at the point where the work would attain its completeness, a suppression of history that is necessary in order to guarantee that very completeness.

The suppression of history in Kant's text is thus not confined to the deferral of that part of the text that could properly be entitled "The History of Pure Reason." It is at work in another way in the "cursory sketch" with which Kant fills out ever so slightly the space of the deferred part of the text (A 853–56/B 881–84). In effect, the sketch proposes to thematize the history of metaphysics in reference to three axes, namely, with respect to object, to origin, and to method. It sketches thus what would be an appropriation of that history to a certain systematic configuration. A similar appropriation, yet oriented to a much richer systematic configuration, is rigorously executed in the Transcendental Dialectic. Rather than simply abandoning the history of metaphysics, turning away as Descartes did from the books of that history to the great book of the world and eventually to what could be found inscribed within oneself, Kant undertakes to domesticate that history, to master it in such a way that it becomes ineffective, in such a way as to secure a certain positive detachment from it. This mastery would be accomplished by transposing the history of metaphysics into such purely systematic form that the illusions that have haunted that history and in a sense produced it can be exposed; that is, the variety of that history is to be reduced to a closed system of inferences the dialectical character of which, even if never finally eradicated, becomes at least thoroughly controllable.

The suppression of history operates not only in these particular divisions of the *Critique of Pure Reason* but also, in a certain global way, throughout Kant's text. It operates most powerfully in that metaphorics that haunts the text and that generates the very concept of architectonic. The metaphorics is of course architectural, and it governs the orientation and the most general articulation of the *Critique of Pure Reason*. The project is to prepare for the construction of the edifice of metaphysics. Such preparation requires, first, a Transcendental Doctrine of Elements, which provides "an estimate of the materials" and determines "for what sort of edifice and for what height and strength of building they suffice," and, second, a Transcendental Doctrine of Method, which projects "the plan" of the edifice (A 707/B 735). And yet, both these forms of preparation presuppose another, one to which Kant orients his project from the very outset: the *Critique of Pure Reason* is to prepare the *ground* on which a system of pure reason, that is, the edifice of metaphysics proper, can be securely built. In Kant's words, it is "to clear and level a ground that is completely overgrown" (*einen ganz verwach-senen Boden zu reinigen und zu ebnen*) (A xxi). What is this overgrowth that has covered the ground of metaphysics and that is to be cleared away by critique? It is metaphysics itself in those guises previously assumed—that is, the history of metaphysics. This wild metaphysics, this metaphysics that has sprung up by nature, that can spring up because metaphysics is, in Kant's phrase, a *"natural* disposition"—this metaphysical overgrowth is to be cut back and cleared away, in order that a quite different metaphysics might replace it, a metaphysics to be produced not by nature but by art, by an art akin to those of the architect and the builder. There is no indication that in clearing away the overgrowth one might come across certain materials that the Transcendental Doctrine of Elements might subsequently propose for use in the construction of the new metaphysical edifice.

But it is not only, not even primarily, a matter of something that has grown out of and over the ground. For the word *verwachsene*, which Kant uses to describe the condition of the ground prior to critique, can mean not only *overgrown* but also *deformed, misshapen, distorted*. How might the ground have been deformed? What deformity might natural metaphysics, the history of metaphysics, have produced in it? Kant's answer shifts the focus of the metaphorics to the underground: metaphysics has dug mole-tunnels. This answer occurs at a point in Kant's text where he has just completed an extended account of Plato's alleged teaching regarding ideas and of the peculiar merit that that teaching has with regard to the principles of morality, legislation, and religion. Granting that such matters are what gives philosophy its peculiar dignity, Kant then abruptly turns against that history to which he had almost accorded a positive role, sets critique against it:

Though the following out of these considerations is what gives to philosophy its peculiar dignity, we must instead occupy ourselves now with a less resplendent, but still meritorious task, namely, to level the ground and make it firm enough for those majestic moral edifices; in this ground are to be found all kinds of mole-tunnels [*allerei Maulwurfsgänge*] that reason has dug in its futile but confident search for treasures and that make that structure precarious." [A 319/B 375–76]

Reason, metaphysics, searches for treasures—for those principles of morality, legislation, and religion that give it its dignity, its worth. It searches by tunneling along beneath the ground, blindly following its natural disposition, oblivious to the network of other tunnels except perhaps for those crossings that, taken collectively, render metaphysics, as Kant says, a battleground of endless controversies. The search is futile; rather than turning up the treasures sought the tunneling only deforms the ground, tunnels it out, rendering it unfit to serve as a site on which secure moral edifices could be erected. Critique is, then, to compensate for the mole-tunneling, to repair the deformed ground, to make it again firm. It is to level the ground—that is, to make the tunnels of reason cave in on themselves. The history of metaphysics is thus to be effectively revoked, suppressed. In this context, however, Kant does not indicate what might be required positively for this restoration of the ground.

However, such an indication, integrated into the same metaphorics, is explicit elsewhere—in the Preface to the *Critique of Judgment:*

For if such a system is one day to be erected under the general name of metaphysics . . . , the ground for this edifice must in advance be explored by critique as deep down as the foundation of the power of principles independent of experience, in order that it may not sink in any part, for this would inevitably bring about the collapse of the whole. [5:168]

In order to prepare the ground, critique must explore that ground all the way down to the bedrock, the foundation. Kant identifies that foundation as founding, preeminently, the power of principles independent of experience—that is, the foundation is just reason itself and critique a critique of reason.

I have assembled this series of passages, all set within the same metaphorics, in order through their mutual attractions and repulsions to release the movement within that metaphorics itself. In the series reason has undergone various metamorphoses: at first a builder, then a natural disposition, then a mole-like searcher for treasures, finally bedrock. The works of reason, the history of metaphysics, has correspondingly become, first, a structure in ruins, then, rank overgrowth, then, a network of mole-tunnels. Yet beneath these transformations there is still another movement, enforced by a set of questions that need now to be made explicit.

According to the last of the passages assembled, critique is to prepare the ground for metaphysics by exploring that ground all the way down to the foundation. This metaphorical exploration of the depths collides with a certain feature of another of the passages—that is, the two, taken together in their opposition, generate a question: How can critique explore the ground all the way down to the bedrock except by tunneling down to it in a way not unlike that very mole-tunneling whose effects critique would expunge? In this case one may then well ask: Can critique successfully dispense with that training in mole-tunneling offered it by the history of metaphysics?—that is, can it sustain the suppression of that history? But suppose indeed that critique tunnels down to the bedrock? At what cost? Does not the mole-tunnel dug by critique compromise precisely what critique above all would accomplish? Does not the critical mole-tunnel too deprive the ground of its firmness, tunnel it out, and threaten the security of any edifices that might be erected on that ground? Or, to transpose the question, how can reason be so divided that on the one hand it tunnels along, mole-like, near the surface, yet on the other hand can be identified with that bedrock to which only critique would penetrate? Especially in this last question a certain fissure begins to open up in the metaphorics. The limits of that metaphorics are thus announced—not, however, limits of the kind that would merely limit the metaphoric system, separating it from another system that it would imperfectly signify. On the contrary, it is a matter of a fissure within the *Critique of*

Pure Reason as a whole, a fissure, a spacing, that makes of it a radically heterogeneous text. And the limits announced by that fissure delimit, divide, that text into different, mostly discordant levels. They make of it a text composed of variously configured leaves, which, sewn (or, rather, basted) together by the thread of the text, could never be bound into a uniform volume.

b | The fissure that has begun to show in the metaphorics of the *Critique of Pure Reason* founds a dynamics. Because this fissure would cleave a unity that cannot but be reasserted as unity, it installs a torsion and a movement within that torsion, a movement generated by the torsion. It is a dyadically structured movement: on the one side, a distorting, that is, an untwisting, a twisting apart, a twisting in two, hence, a twisting out of shape, even a perverting; on the other side, a contorting, that is, a twisting together, hence, an imperfect and precarious reestablishing of unity. Certain phases of this movement are already outlined by the questions that have been broached: for example, the distortion of reason into depth and surface, bedrock and mole-tunnel, which are then contorted, twisted together, into that critical mole-tunneling down to the bedrock; in turn, such critical mole-tunneling is untwisted into an establishing of an absolutely firm but subterranean foundation, the bedrock, and, on the other hand, a new tunneling out under the site on which the edifice of metaphysics would be erected.

In order to begin showing that the fissure and the dynamics opened in the metaphorics of the *Critique of Pure Reason* secretly permeate the text in its entirety, let me now set that metaphorics aside, at least temporarily, and attempt to trace the same fissure in a context quite remote from the metaphorics.

From the various formulations of the general critical problem let me choose that formulation that predominates in the Preface to the first edition of the *Critique of Pure Reason*—the formulation of the critical problem as the problem of the unity of reason. According to this formulation, pure reason is a perfect unity—"so perfect a unity," as Kant says, that it can generate no question to which it would be ultimately insufficient. And yet, this unity, perfect though it be, is problematic, even threatened. For there occurs, to use Kant's precise phrase, "Missverstand der Vernunft mit ihr selbst" (A xii). The phrase has two senses, both audible in the English word "misunderstanding": on the one hand, misunderstanding by reason *of* itself, in the sense of its being in error, being deceived, about itself; on the other hand, misunderstanding by reason *with* itself, in the sense of disagreement, dissension, conflict, with itself. The second sense recalls Kant's description of metaphysics, a few pages earlier, as a battlefield of endless controversies—controversies that are now to be settled not on the battlefield but in a court of law, before that tribunal that Kant would institute. It is clear now why the work of reason, the history of metaphysics, lies in ruins: it is a battlefield. One can only wonder, however, what arcane transformation has converted mole-tunneling (down to the bedrock) into a court of law. But let me again put the metaphorics aside.

Reason, so perfect a unity, falls nevertheless into misunderstanding—misunderstanding in the two senses indicated, senses that, internally communicating, merge in the concept of a disruption of reason's perfect unity with itself. The critical problem is, then, to resolve this disruption so as to restore reason to that condition of unity proper to it. Critique would repair the fissure; taking the side of contortion, it would twist reason back together with itself.

But what provokes the misunderstanding of reason, the disruption of its otherwise essential unity? What sets it against itself? A passage in the Preface to the second edition provides a decisive clue. Referring to those principles in connection with which reason is set against itself, Kant writes: "They threaten actually to extend over everything the boundaries of sensibility, to which they properly belong, and so to displace the pure (practical) employment of reason" (B xxiv–v). The disruption has, thus, to do with a certain infringement by sensibility, an infringement on reason, an infringement that, displacing reason, sets it against itself.

Despite the threat posed to the unity of reason, that unity is proper to reason, is an essential unity. As such it has a twofold methodological significance for the *Critique of Pure Reason.* In the first place, this essential unity makes it possible for a critique of reason to achieve completeness: "It can therefore finish its work and bequeath it to posterity as capital to which no addition can be made" (B xxiv). It is even obliged to achieve such completeness, and in fact Kant explicitly lays claim to having achieved it: "In this undertaking I have made completeness my chief aim, and I venture to assert that there is not a single metaphysical problem that has not been solved or for the solution of which the key at least has not been supplied" (A xiii). Significantly, the very next sentence is the one in which reason is characterized as "so perfect a unity"—significantly because it is precisely this unity, this being one with itself, being self-enclosed, importing nothing "from without," nothing external and contingent that might render the account of it intrinsically incomplete—it is from the unity of reason in this sense that the possibility, even the necessity, of completeness originates. Kant is explicit: "I have to do merely with reason itself and its pure thinking, for the complete knowledge of which I need not seek far around me, since I come upon them in my own self" (A xiv).

The other, much more far reaching methodological significance of the unity of reason is already broached by Kant's reference to coming upon reason within oneself. Specifically, this other significance corresponds to the concept of unity as self-presence, that is, to the conception of reason's unity as oneness with itself in the sense of presence to itself. The significance of such presence becomes clear as soon as one reads the genitive expression "critique *of* reason" both subjectively and objectively: reason is both subject and object of the critique. In other words, the critique is reason's investigation of itself, a matter of self-knowledge—or, in Kant's words, "a call to reason to undertake anew the most difficult of all its tasks, namely, that of self-knowledge" (A xi). This task of self-knowledge can be undertaken only on the basis of a certain presence to self, a presence of reason to itself. The unity of reason, reason's presence to itself, is a condition of the very possibility of a critique of reason. And this presence as well as the self-knowledge that it makes possible would seem, by Kant's account, quite unlimited, essentially complete. Referring to the task as that of "the *inventory* of all our possessions through pure reason," Kant writes: "Here nothing can escape us, since that which reason produces entirely out of itself cannot be concealed but is brought to light by reason itself as soon as the common principle has been discovered" (A xx).

The traces of fissure can now be indicated—three traces of fissure, of distortion, of spacing, within what is most remote from all metaphorics, reason itself. First, reason is essentially one; and yet, in misunderstanding it can be set against itself, can become twofold (as Kant will most graphically show in the antinomy of pure reason). One may of course insist that this fissure of one into two is merely accidental, that reason remains *essentially* one; but then it will be difficult to avoid granting also that this essence is a remote one—aloof, incredibly, from the entire history of metaphysics, which remained merely the battleground of the indeterminately dyadic. Second, reason is self-enclosed, importing nothing from without; and yet, it can be infringed upon and even displaced from its proper self-enclosure—infringed upon by its other, sensibility. Here again one could isolate the distortion as merely accidental only at the cost of an incredible suppression not so much directly of sensibility itself as rather of the historical testimony to the infringement, the testimony provided by the history of metaphysics—to say nothing of the testimony constituted by the *Critique of Pure Reason* itself, by the metaphorics installed at least on the edge of critical reason itself. Third, reason is self-present, one with itself in the sense of unlimited presence to itself; and yet, there can occur misunderstanding in which reason is deceived about itself, concealed from itself, separated by ignorance from itself. Does one dare to make of self-ignorance a mere accident and of the god at Delphi a dispensable herald of mere accident? Does one dare to suppress the very origin of philosophy?

C   Let me now shift from this preparatory phase of general formulations, the phase of the Prefaces and the Introduction, to the phase with which the *Critique of Pure Reason* properly begins, the Transcendental Aesthetic. In this first major phase of critique one can already discern quite clearly the line of the fissure within critical reason.

The very title "Transcendental Aesthetic" borders on paradox. As transcendental, this phase shares with all other phases of the Transcendental Doctrine of Elements a directedness to those elements in human knowledge that are a priori, that is, those elements that are not derived from without but ultimately from within, from the subject itself. On the other hand, as an aesthetic, this phase is directed to αἴσθησις, sensibility, the capacity for reception from without, a capacity that would *seem* to be turned completely outward, lacking any inward reserve from which a priori elements might originate. It is precisely this *seeming* that is challenged by the Transcendental Aesthetic: not only does it delimit in a general fashion a formal order-giving component within sensibility, *pure* intuition within *empirical* intuition, but also it exhibits the elements that constitute that formal component. Or rather, beginning with certain elements, namely, space and time, it demonstrates that they are precisely such as to constitute an inward, order-giving side of intuition, that they are *pure intuitions*.

Let me focus on the first of the two remarkably symmetrical sections into which the Transcendental Aesthetic is divided, the sections devoted to space, and, more narrowly, on the first of the three subsections into which this section is divided, the subsection to which in the second edition Kant added the title "Metaphysische Erörterung dieses Begriffs" (Metaphysical exposition of this concept). If one chose to attend to the root of the central word in this title, to the *Ort* in *Erörterung,* the title could then be read as proposing to set the concept of space in its *place,* to put it where it belongs, in its proper *space.* A curious operation indeed: putting space within a space to which it has in advance a proprietary relation—curious especially because it is an operation hardly proper to reason, an operation that, immersed in intuition, at least in metaphor, could not but pervert reason, turning even critical reason against itself, tunneling out the ground beneath that site that critique would prepare. In any case— putting the metaphorics again aside—this placing is to be metaphysical, that is, space is to be placed on the side of the metaphysical, in the region of the a priori. Space is to be expounded as a priori, not as an a priori concept but rather as an inward, a priori, component of sensibility. It is to be expounded as a priori (or pure) *intuition*—in Kant's words, "as given a priori." Thus is prescribed the organization of that set of four individual expositions that constitute the metaphysical exposition as a whole: the first two are devoted to showing that space is a priori, the other two to showing that it is an intuition, not a concept.

Let me narrow the focus still more and consider only the first of the four expositions. Actually this exposition occupies a very crucial position: as the first of the four, it is located at the beginning of the first subsection of the first section of the first part of the *Critique of Pure Reason*; and, strictly speaking, that is, in terms of the topology of the entire work, everything preceding it is merely preparatory. In other words, this exposition is the opening move of the *Critique of Pure Reason.* It needs to be read carefully:

Space is not an empirical concept that has been derived from outer experiences. For in order that certain sensations be re- ferred to something outside me (i.e., to something in another region of space [*Orte des Raumes*] from that in which I find myself), and similarly in order that I may be able to represent [*vorstellen*] them as outside and alongside one another, hence as not merely different but as in different places [*in verschiedenen Orten*] the representation of space must be presupposed [*dazu*

muss die Vorstellung des Raumes schon zum Grunde liegen]. Therefore, the representation of space cannot be obtained by experience from the relations of outer appearances, but rather this
outer experience is itself possible at all only through that representation. [A 23/B 38].

The formal structure of this exposition is clearly marked. The
first and third of the three sentences that compose it merely
state the thesis being demonstrated, the first stating it in
negative form, the third both negatively and then also positively. The second sentence presents the demonstration
proper—or, rather, the two complementary demonstrations
marked by the parallel construction of its conditional clause.
One demonstration proceeds from the representation of
things as themselves spatially related: in order for one to be
able to represent things as outside and alongside one another,
the representation of space must be presupposed, must
already underlie that representing of things, must provide its
ground (*muss . . . schon zum Grunde liegen*). Since the representation of relations between things thus presupposes the
representation of space, the representation of space cannot
have been obtained by abstraction from the relations between
things, cannot have been obtained empirically at all. The
other demonstration proceeds from the very possibility of
outer representation: in order to be able to represent objects
as outside oneself, in some region outside oneself, that region, the outside as such, space itself, must already be
represented.

The structure of the demonstrations can be focused more
sharply. In both cases a certain actual, hence possible, representational activity is posited: in one case, the representation
of things as spatially distinct from one another; in the other
case, the representation of things as spatially distinct from
oneself. The two demonstrations are thus quite complementary, one positing the representation of spatial dis-
tinctness between objects, the other that of spatial distinct-
ness between subject and object. Putting them again
together into a single demonstration, one may say that the

demonstration begins by positing (in both its moments) the representation of things as spatially distinct. It is a matter, then, of positing another representational activity as ground of the possibility of the activity initially posited—that is, the demonstration traces an intrinsic order of grounding between two representational activities, the representation of things as spatially distinct and the representation of space as such. The demonstration (*de-monstrare*) shows, makes manifest (*monstrare*), this intrinsic order, so that from (*de*) it, on the ground that it provides, the a priori character of space can be established.

The entire force of the demonstration derives, then, from the showing of the relevant order of grounding. Where does this showing occur? Certainly not in that text cited earlier, that text that one might otherwise identify with the demonstration itself. For that text *only outlines* the order of grounding, that is, *asserts* that if one is to be able to represent objects as spatially distinct, one must already have represented space as such. The text merely posits the order of grounding, thereby inviting from elsewhere, from outside the text, the showing of the order of grounding as proper to the terms thus connected. In what region could this deferred showing occur? Only in that region to which belong those terms to which the order of grounding is to be shown to be proper. But those terms are representational activities, and so the region of the showing can only be that of representational activity as such, that is, subjectivity, and the showing thus a reflexive showing, a self-showing, a showing of oneself to oneself. In other words, the entire demonstration hinges ultimately on a certain reflective presence to one's own representational powers, a reflective presence to which it could become manifest that certain representational activities are grounded on others, that, specifically, the representation of things as spatially distinct is grounded on the representation of space as such. In the end, the demonstration of the order of grounding is itself grounded on the subject's presence to itself.

The opening move of the *Critique of Pure Reason* thus

silently incorporates a tunneling down to a ground constituted by self-presence. In this way it rejoins the preparatory
phase, regresses (at least in part) to the Preface (to the first
edition); for it was precisely the positing of self-presence,
specifically of the presence of reason to itself, that was found
to dominate that Preface. In a sense the Preface posited that
self-presence as ground—not, however, as ground firmly
established but rather as ground threatened by deformity, as
tunneled out and thus made infirm. Indeed it is precisely this
condition of the ground that generates the need for a critique
capable of restoring firmness to that ground.

The fissure in critical reason is now unmistakable: in its
opening move toward restoring the ground it cannot but
plant itself upon that very ground—that is, the bedrock to
which it would tunnel down is identical with the ground that
that bedrock would support and make firm, the ground
tunneled out by the history of metaphysics. Undertaking to
restore the ground by planting itself on that very ground—
this expresses the torsion installed by the fissure opened
between metaphysical reason and critical reason. That torsion twists reason itself, installs within it a movement of
contortion and distortion—untwisting and then twisting
together again metaphysical reason and critical reason, the
tunneled-out ground and the bedrock. The bedrock is thus
itself set in motion—that is, there is no bedrock. Critical
reason cannot isolate itself more than temporarily from the
threat of history, cannot once and for all suppress its history.

d | I have deliberately passed over certain distinctions and cor-
respondingly necessary qualifications and instead proceeded
directly from the tunneling out exposed in the opening of the
Critique of Pure Reason to the fissure, torsion, and movement
in the work as a whole—passed them over because the
ground that they would invoke could eventually be exposed
as equally tunneled out. Let me mention two such distinctions and sketch very briefly some of the complications that
they introduce.

The demonstration with which the *Critique of Pure Reason* opens was found to be grounded on the subject's presence to itself. That ground was then identified with the ground to which the Preface had been addressed. But in fact there is a difference that ought to limit this identification: the difference between *reason's* presence to itself, invoked by the Preface, and the *subject's* presence to itself. This difference is (at least within the framework of theoretical knowledge) constituted by the existence of a mode of the subject's presence to itself contained in that other stem of human knowledge that Kant opposes to reason. Account must be taken of the subject's presence to itself in inner intuition.

The second distinction concerns the difference between the Preface and the work proper—that is, the difference between their respective ways of taking up the issue of the deformity of reason, of the disruption of its self-presence. In the Preface the deformity of reason is merely posited; that positing has of course a ground, namely, the glance back at the ruins left by the history of metaphysics; but, granted the turn from history to reason, granted the suppression of history, this ground must be declared no *critical* ground at all. And so, within critique the deformity of reason must eventually be reestablished on a critical ground. Consequently, the expedient that I have used, that of regressing to the Preface, to its historically grounded positing of the deformity of reason, would eventually need to be replaced by recourse to those phases of the *Critique of Pure Reason* in which the critical grounding is carried through. And yet, such recourse, this hermeneutical tunneling, would itself then only repeat that very movement from history to reason that it would call into question. Thus placing itself in question, it could never simply replace but only complement the glance back at the history of metaphysics.

Initially, however, this recourse would need to be isolated from the complications of such complementarity, and focused on those phases of critique at which presence to self is delimited at the levels of intuition, understanding, and practical reason. It would need to show how these three delimitations, taken together as exhaustive, so radically limit presence to self as to confirm that disruption that in the Preface was posited on merely historical grounds. It would thus mark in requisite detail the lines, the total configuration, of that torsion by which the entire *Critique of Pure Reason* is shaken from the ground up and thrown finally out of joint: critique withdraws that very self-presence that its possibility as critique requires—that is, it revokes itself. But that revocation is itself unstable, presupposing what it would revoke—that is, the revocation must in turn be itself revoked. Thus it is a matter not so much of a structure being thrown out of joint as rather of its being set in movement— or, more precisely, of its being transformed into a movement of mutually determining self-presence and withdrawal of self-presence, a movement of contortion and distortion, a play of self-delimitation, a spacing.

And yet, this play would remain empty, could never become a play in which, however veiledly, however playfully, there would occur a manifestation, were there not a certain opening of reason to itself. Such an opening, an opening within reason, an establishing of distance from oneself, is precisely what is accomplished in every recovery of tradition. The *Critique of Pure Reason* would of course forgo such recovery except as something merely preparatory, rigorously excluded from critique proper; it would suppress its history, set itself against and over against that history. How little it succeeds, however, in actually maintaining that stance is manifest at every turn of the work—for example, by the way in which the ontological determinations of space and time in the Transcendental Aesthetic are governed by the traditional categorial schema, by the way in which the clue for the discovery of the categories is taken to lie in the traditional table of judgments, by the way in which the typology of dialectical inference follows the lines not only of the traditional theory of the syllogism but also of traditional metaphysics at large. Indeed that critical reason traced in the *Critique of Pure Reason* could hardly be less self-enclosed, less isolated from the history of metaphysics, unless it were simply to abandon entirely its assumed stance against that history. At every turn that history, eluding the critical defense, silently encroaches on its ground, invades its very core, and precisely thereby opens it to itself, giving content to its play of self-delimitation. On the other hand, that opening to itself provides the space in which critical reason can establish its distance from its history—not, however, at a single stroke, not in an absolute turn away from history, but rather only in those successive stages marked out by the interplay of critique and history, appropriation and disavowal, only by critically playing through the content of that history. In turn, this play of distancing weaves into the text strands of varying determinacy, more or less emptily taken over from tradition, more or less redetermined and systematically appropriated. The texture of the *Critique of Pure Reason* is exceptionally variegated, and its reading requires, correspondingly, a hermeneutics capable of tracing its heterogeneous threads, a hermeneutics capable of reenacting this play of form, a hermeneutics both formal and playful.

This concept of history is to be rigorously contrasted with that which Kant himself explicitly developed in his "Idea for a Universal History from a Cosmopolitan Point of View," contrasted in terms both of function and of locus. What Kant explicitly develops is a practical concept of history, history understood in relation to human action. Focusing primarily on the side of the discipline, in distinction from what that discipline would take as its theme, Kant characterizes history as the narration of the appearances of freedom in nature. As such, history attempts to discern, from the standpoint of the whole, a progressive realization of man's capacities, a development toward those general conditions (civic society) that make such realization possible. History, by narrating the story of this realization, also contributes to it, belongs to the story it narrates. By contrast, that history that I have sought to expose at work within the *Critique of Pure Reason* is such as to disrupt the very distinction in terms of which the practical concept of history is developed, the distinction between discipline and theme. For the history secretly operating in the critical text is a certain handing over. Most narrowly, it is a matter of history as handing over certain conceptual and linguistic structures in which one is thus always already engaged—already engaged, for example, whenever one sets about studying history, practicing the discipline of history. More comprehensively, it is a matter of history as handing over the very space of reason's self-presence. In Kant's essay on history there is no more than a hint of such a concept: this hint occurs when Kant insists that reason, progressing "from one level of insight to another" only by means of "trial, practice, and instruction," requires (in view of the short span of human life) a "series of generations, each of which passes its own enlightenment to its successors . . ." (8:19). But Kant neither develops this hint nor brings it to bear on philosophy itself. The contrast between the two concepts of history is also one of locus. Kant's explicitly developed concept of history is intra-systematic: history recounts man's transition from nature to that moral culture possible only in civic society; and so, like art, it pertains to the mediation between nature and freedom, having thus the same systematic locus as the issues of the *Critique of Judgment*. By contrast, the other concept of history is extrasystematic—or, rather, to the extent that it proves to be in play within a system that would exclude it, it disrupts the very distinction between "inside" and "outside." In decentering reason, it disrupts the very concept of system.

Eventually critical reason would need to be opened in another direction also, in the direction of sensibility as well as that of history; or, rather, that opening would need to be made explicit, for indeed within the *Critique of Pure Reason* critical reason is already invaded by sensibility, its alleged self-enclosedness shattered beyond repair. In fact, Kant explicitly thematizes such an encroachment by sensibility at the level of understanding, establishing precisely such encroachment as the sole condition under which pure concepts of the understanding can acquire objective validity. And, at least at the preparatory level of the Preface, he refers almost explicitly to a corresponding, though disruptive, encroachment at the level of reason. On the other hand, he nowhere even alludes to a positively effective encroachment of sensibility upon reason—at least not in the *Critique of Pure Reason*, which for Kant is marked off from that blending of reason and sensibility that the *Critique of Judgment* can permit, rigidly marked off by the distinction between philosophy and art. In particular, the *Critique of Pure Reason* allows at the thematic level no space whatsoever for that positive encroachment of sensibility upon reason, that sensibilization of reason, that takes place in metaphor. Much less does it thematically open within critical reason the space for a metaphorics, a metaphorics that, thus located, would assume the form of a metaphorics of reason, a metaphorics in which what would be metaphorized would be reason itself—metaphorized, for example, as tunneling. I have tried, on the other hand, to give some indication of how thoroughly the critical reason traced in the *Critique of Pure Reason* does indeed harbor a metaphorics and of how, consequently, a reading of that text requires not only a hermeneutics but also a poetics.

Yet here, no less than in the case of history, the torsion would remain in force, for reason is opposed to sensibility and, correspondingly remote from metaphor, can never cease to expunge its metaphorics, to take distance from it. The torsion is such that the metaphorics could never completely dominate the labor of critical reason—or, rather, it is such as to transform that labor into a play of mutually limiting reason and metaphor.

These transformations of a rigid subterranean edifice into a rigorously structured movement of self-delimitation, these transformations of a self-enclosed labor of reason into an open play of reason and history, reason and sensibility—these transformations, these releasings of spacings, could hardly be broached without also bringing into question as a whole that particular metaphorics that, generating the architectonic, the very concept of architectonic, comes so near dominating the *Critique of Pure Reason* and making of its play of self-delimitation a labor of grounding. The transformations broached prompt a new metaphorics fitted to an architecture that would require no ground, no final bedrock, an architecture not of rigid edifices but of moving, self-developing forms—a metaphorics that would be more musical than architectural, a hymn to pure reason.

Recall again the initial Socratic context, a critical context, the context in which Socrates faces the absolute crisis, death. It is within this context that Socrates, turning back to his own history, tells of that turn that was eventually to become the turn from history and sensibility to reason. Recall now that other turn made by Socrates in this same critical context, his turn to the practice of music, a practice begun with a hymn to Apollo and consummated in a great myth of the earth.

2 | HOVERINGS —

Imagination and the Spacing of Truth

Reason is also a dove.

One can trace in Kant's text the transformation of the metaphorics of ground into one of flight. It occurs in that part of the Introduction where Kant first introduces the problem of metaphysics, the problem of the possibility and limits of a mode of knowledge that would "leave the field of all possible experience" (A 2–3/B 6), that would "soar far above the teachings of experience" (B xiv). Kant first suggests that it is a matter of transition from one kind of ground to another, a transition that has the appearance of being natural:

Now it does indeed seem natural that, as soon as we have left the ground of experience, we should, through careful inquiries, assure ourselves as to the foundations [*Grundlegung*] of any building that we propose to erect. . . . [A 3/B 7]

It would be a matter of considering how the other ground, reason itself, can suffice for supporting the edifice of metaphysics. Such consideration would be natural; indeed nothing could be more natural "if by the word 'natural' we signify what fittingly and reasonably ought to happen" (A 4/B 7–8). If the natural were the rational, if reason governed what happens by nature, then there would always have been critique, as long as metaphysics itself. But the equation does not hold; on the contrary, it is precisely the inequality of reason and nature that poses the problem to which critique would respond. For reason exceeds nature; and, at least in the sphere of the "ought," nature resists forcefully the governance of reason. And so what ordinarily happens, what is natural in this sense, is that critical considerations are neglected:

> But if we mean by "natural" what ordinarily happens, then on the contrary nothing is more natural and more intelligible than the fact that this inquiry has been so long neglected. [A 4/B 8]

And yet, it is not only a matter of neglect, of following the natural inclination to regard rational grounds as hardly more questionable than natural grounds, as indeed analogous to the latter. On the contrary, there is indisputable positive testimony to the capacity of reason genuinely to exceed natural knowledge, a sure testimony to the validity of certain modes of purely rational knowledge. Especially because of the example of mathematical knowledge, the capacity of reason to exceed nature, the possibility of a rational knowledge that radically surpasses natural knowledge rather than being a mere analogical extension of it—such excess of reason over nature is all too easily taken for granted, and such critical consideration as would call that excess into question is then all too readily forgone: "Misled [*eingenommen*; in A: *aufgemuntert* (encouraged)] by such a proof of the power of reason, the demand for the extension [of knowledge] recognizes no limits" (A 5–6/B 8).

For critique it is this excess that is preeminently the problem. And it is this excess of reason over nature—the problem of this excess—that broaches the other metaphorics. Reason assumes the guise of something eminently natural:

> The light dove, cleaving the air in her free flight and feeling its resistance, might suppose [*könnte die Vorstellung fassen*] that its flight would be still easier [lit.: would succeed much better (*noch viel besser gelingen werde*)] in empty space. It was thus that Plato left the world of the senses, as setting too narrow limits to the understanding, and ventured out beyond it on the wings of the ideas, in the empty space of the pure understanding. He did not observe that with all his efforts he made no advance, meeting no resistance that might, as it were, serve as a support upon which he could take a stand, to which he could apply his powers, and so set his understanding in motion. [A 5/B 8–9]

The Platonic dove, metaphysics, would soar off into the beyond, abandoning thereby precisely what makes its flight possible, the supporting medium. Note how readily Kant converts this medium into a ground, how easily therefore he can revert here to the metaphorics of ground—most obtrusively in the immediately following sentence: "It is, indeed, the common fate of human reason to complete its speculative edifices as speedily as possible and only afterward to inquire whether their foundations [*der Grund dazu*] are reliable." And yet, the two metaphorics do not simply coalesce. What is required of the Platonic dove is not a ground upon which to take a stand. What is required is not that the dove desist from flight but only that it be disciplined not to soar off—or to try to soar off—into the beyond. What is required is that it remain in that space between earth and heaven, that instead of soaring into the beyond it learn to hover above the earth.

What does such hovering require? How must reason be determined in order that it be capable of such hovering? Or, more precisely, what displacement must reason undergo in order to learn to hover?

a   Reason is set in movement, into a movement of hovering, in Fichte's *Wissenschaftslehre*.[1] This displacement is not regarded by Fichte as a break with Kant; quite the contrary, he insists that his entire system "is nothing other than the Kantian," that it contains "the same view of things but is in method quite independent of the Kantian presentation [*es enthält dieselbe Ansicht der Sache, ist aber in seinem Verfahren ganz unabhängig von der Kantischen Darstellung*]" (1:420). This identity has been contested ever since it was proclaimed; indeed one of the first to contest it was Kant himself.[2] And yet, however contestable it may be if taken straightforwardly (and with all the presuppositions required in order to take it straightforwardly), the identity becomes, on the other hand, highly provocative, *fragwürdig* in the positive sense, once the movement within the critical system is released; for the movement is such as to efface the otherwise strict distinction between the view of things and the procedure by which that view would be developed or presented, that is, between theory and method, between *Sache* and *Darstellung*.

Still, there is, to be sure, a difference in method, in presentation, certain differences that serve to bring Fichte's text closer to a certain threshold. Most significant in this regard is the way in which Fichte's text (de)limits the philosophical text as such. The (de)limitation occurs on the threshold of the philosophical text, in a retrospective introduction.

The *First Introduction to the Wissenschaftslehre* (1798) begins:

Attend to yourself: turn your gaze away from everything that surrounds you, turn it inward [*in dein Inneres*]—this is the first demand that philosophy makes of its disciple. It is a matter of discourse [*Es ist . . . die Rede*] not about anything that lies outside you but only about yourself [*von dir selbst*]. [1:422]

The text begins at the beginning, at the beginning of philosophy, with that radical break with which philosophy begins: a break with one's ordinary comportment toward things, a turning of one's attention, one's gaze, away from things back upon oneself.

The rhetorical character of this initiatory text is quite marked. It begins in the imperative rather than the indicative and then—after the dash—makes the transition to the indicative only in order to indicate that what has just been said imperatively is the founding imperative of philosophy, "the first demand that philosophy makes of its disciple." Then comes another self-indication: the text indicates that it is text, discourse (*Rede*), in distinction from what the discourse is about. This self-indication is then linked up with still another, with one of quite a different order: the text is *von dir selbst*; it is *about yourself*, in the direct address of the text, or *about oneself*, in a form of address that would at least feign more detachment and indirection. And yet, as imperative the text is also addressed to the "you," to oneself, demanding of oneself the turn to oneself. It is, furthermore, a text that bears a signature and that—especially as imperative, even more markedly when the text more explicitly inclines toward first person—carries a reference to an authorial I, to an I that, from outside the text, speaks in the text, to an I at the edge of the text. The text is thus woven between three terms, stretched, as it were, between them: the I who speaks, the you to whom the discourse is addressed, and the you to whom the latter is commanded to turn. Hence, the (de)limitation of the text: it is (de)limited by these three terms all of which fall outside or at the edge of the text, or which, rather, define the edge of the Fichtean text. In the (de)limitation there is a dynamics, one that mirrors the dynamics of the system that the text would present. The imperative demands a turn to oneself, a certain (re)unity with oneself. It demands it in the *familiar* form of the second person: *Merke auf dich selbst*—almost as though the demand were addressed to oneself. Indeed, in the end it is to be so addressed—that is, the dynamics is such as to orient the operation of the text to a peculiar merging of the I who speaks in the text (from without) and the you to whom is addressed the demand *Merke auf dich selbst*—a merging that would be both a withdrawal of the authorial I and an assumption of his voice by the you to whom the imperative is addressed. The you is to appropriate the demand, to place the demand upon himself, ceasing thereby to function as a you, affirming most authentically that it is an I—or, rather, not even just *an* I but simply: I.[3] Thus, in the end, the terms between which the text is stretched would prove to coalesce—that is, the (de)limitation of the text, the text itself, would prove to be only a provisional requirement. It would always have to give way to a space of *enactment* and could at most only be temporarily reinscribed in that space, or rather at its threshold, as outward reminder of inward deeds. The Fichtean text as such is limited to the threshold, is not yet philosophy, not even the beginning of philosophy.

Little wonder, then, that at the threshold of this threshold, in the Preface to the *Grundlage der gesammten Wissenschaftslehre*, Fichte finds it "necessary to recall that I do not say everything but have also wished to leave to my reader something to think about" (1:89). It is not a matter of an author willfully, even perhaps a bit maliciously, withholding certain truths that he could have conveyed to his readers. On the contrary, Fichte well understood that he *could not* have said everything, that he could not have produced a discourse capable of assuming the role of enactment. It is a matter of truths that no text could ever convey, of truths that one can only convey to oneself, precisely because they are the truths of one's relation to oneself.

Little wonder, then, that Fichte insists that

> what sort of philosophy one chooses depends, therefore, on what sort of man one is; for a philosophical system is not a dead piece of furniture that we can reject or accept as we wish; it is rather a thing animated by the soul of the man who holds it. [1:434]

Need it be said that here it is not a matter of any kind of relativism; least of all is it some kind of reduction of philosophy to autobiography. It is rather a matter of the limits of the philosophical text and of the necessity of enactment.

The character of such limitation is developed in Fichte's text "Von der Sprachfähigkeit und dem Ursprunge der Sprache" (1795). This text serves in effect to secure the limits of the philosophical text and to install enactment in a security beyond those limits. More generally, its effect is to provide reason with protection against any intrusion by language that would compromise its inwardness, mixing inside and outside, installing nonreason within reason. This effect becomes evident in the very way in which Fichte's text poses the problem of language: it is a matter, first, of discovering the drive by which man is impelled toward the realization of language and then, second, of projecting on that basis an a priori history of language. According to Fichte, the relevant drive stems from the highest principle in man, namely, the imperative: be always at one with yourself (*sey immer einig mit dir selbst*). The drive to such at-oneness issues in the effort to subdue nonrational nature so as to bring it into correspondence with reason; but in the case of an object in which rationality is already expressed, the drive is, instead, toward a reciprocity, and it is in service to this reciprocity—in order to indicate one's thoughts to the other in a definite way—that man is driven to invent language. Thus: "In the drive, grounded in the nature of man, to find rationality outside himself, there lies the particular drive toward realizing a language" (8:309). Accordingly, one could place language among those strategies by which the outside, the other of reason, would be reduced, by which it would be constituted as the outside *of reason* and denied any radical otherness such as could seriously threaten the self-identical interiority of reason.

Fichte appends a note that is even more explicit:

I do not prove here that man cannot think without language or that without it he can have no general abstract concepts. Certainly he can by means of the images that he projects for himself through phantasy [*die er durch die Phantasie sich entwirft*]. It is my conviction that language has been considered much too important when it has been thought that without it no employment of reason would have taken place at all. [8:309n.]

Reason is essentially secured beyond language, however imperative the latter may be in the (self-)development of reason, in its drive to posit itself in its other. Nevertheless, Fichte does not simply appeal to essentiality but rather offers a certain specific security, as it were, for the release of reason from language: beyond language one can still exercise reason by means of the images projected by phantasy. *Imagination* is admitted even into the silent citadel of reason—at a cost that it is precisely my intention to assess.

Outside the citadel imagination is in play everywhere, for Fichte installs it at the very origin of the philosophical text. Recalling the (Socratic) turn from sensible to supersensible—as though it proceeded prelinguistically, as though it had never been a turn to λόγοι—Fichte then undertakes to explain how one comes to invent signs for the spiritual or supersensible concepts that will have been constituted through the turn:

> These signs for supersensible ideas are easily found on the basis of a ground lying in the soul of man. Namely, there is within us a unification of sensible and spiritual representations through the schemata that are brought forth by the imagination. From these schemata designations [*Bezeichnungen*] for spiritual concepts are derived. Specifically, the linguistic sign, which was already had by the sensible object from which the schema was drawn, was itself carried over [*übergetragen*] to the supersensible concept. [8:322]

Without the operation of imagination, without the "metaphorizing" operation of the schemata, the *Übertragung* of sensible signs to supersensible concepts, there would be no signs for the spiritual or supersensible, no philosophical text, but only, at most, the silent citadel, philosophy withdrawn into silence, into the silence of sheer enactment.

Fichte's "Ueber Geist und Buchstab in der Philosophie" (1794; published 1798) outlines in the domain of art an opposition corresponding to that between enactment and philosophical text. Beginning with that single, indivisible drive (*Trieb*) that is the highest principle of activity in man, Fichte distinguishes within it between the cognitive drive, the practical drive, and the aesthetic drive. What sets the aesthetic drive apart from the other two is the fact that it aims not at correspondence between representation and object (such as can be achieved by adjustment of one or the other) but merely at the representation solely for the sake of its determination. Within the sphere of the aesthetic drive, representation is the goal, not correspondence with an object. It is simply a matter of aesthetic images brought forth within man's interiority and belonging to that citadel no less essentially than does enactment. This essential sphere of the aesthetic is to be rigorously distinguished from the *presentation of* aesthetic images outside this sphere, from their duplication, as it were, in sensible form:

It is possible that a presentation of the aesthetic images [*eine Darstellung des ästhetischen Bildes*] is required in the sensible world; however, this comes about not through the aesthetic drive, whose employment terminates completely in the mere projection [*Entwerfung*] of the images within the soul, but rather through the practical drive, which . . . sets up imitations [*Nachbildungen*] in actuality. [8:281]

It is almost the same as with language. At least it is almost the same once the transition has been made from the domain of mere taste to that of spirit and genius, once imagination comes into play in its full freedom: the provision of outer imitations of inner aesthetic images is a means of establishing a reciprocity that, in turn, serves to confirm the essential at-oneness of reason, to confirm that "what is posited through the essence of reason is the same in all rational individuals" (8:292). The establishing of reciprocity is a seeking and a communicating of this common sense (*Gemeinsinn*):

Partly in order to seek this sense in others, partly in order to communicate to them what for him is so attractive, the genius clothes in more stable matter [*in festere Körper*] the forms [*die Gestalten*] that show themselves unveiled to his spiritual eyes, and so sets them before his contemporaries. [8:292]

It is a matter of disposition (*Stimmung*), of the artist's impressing into material form the disposition of his spirit, thus expressing the latter. It is a matter of expressing the common turnings and oscillations of one's inner life and of one's self-active force, something to which even language is inadequate, for, as Fichte insists, "no language has found words for this" (8:294); and so with art it is not entirely the same as with language. It is a matter of artistic activity that fashions an object in such a way that it comes to express the inner movement of the soul. Fichte refers to the example of music in which the artist lets the silent movements within sound in the space without and resound (silently) in the soul of the listener.

Whether it is a question of truth or of art, it is necessary to draw the same rigorous distinction between an essential interiority and a nonessential exteriority in which the essential forms would be outwardly duplicated. Hence, the distinctions form a single series: enactment/text, thought/language, disposition/material expression. In each case it is a matter of the opposition between spirit and letter (*Geist und Buchstab*), an opposition that itself, however, results from a metaphorical broadening of one member of the series (thought/language), from a metaphorizing that reduces the difference between language and music, an operation analogous to song.

There is also a reduction of difference in play between the terms of the oppositions, a free passage between them that cannot but mix what would be rigorously kept apart. Both thought and spirit, truth and art, admit this play, the play of imagination. The theoretical *Wissenschaftslehre*, retracing systematically the *Critique of Pure Reason*, will demonstrate the necessity of admitting this play into the space of enactment.

In any case, philosophy and art, articulated by the same opposition, are also convergent in their aims. The aesthetic drive aims at nothing outside of man but only at something within (8:283). Its aim thus converges with that of the cognitive drive once the latter carries out the turn from things back to the I. Beyond the point at which the turn is made one could no longer isolate art from truth, aesthetic drive from cognitive drive; indeed Fichte marks these limits of the distinction by insisting on the indivisibility of the fundamental drive. And so, though Fichte's epistolary text "Ueber Geist und Buchstab in der Philosophie," breaking off after the third letter, deals with the spirit and the letter only in art and not in philosophy,[4] the transition from the former to the latter is thoroughly prepared by the fragmentary text, which one could easily piece together with other texts (such as the *Introductions* of 1798) that would essentially complete it by adding to the opposition that articulates art the corresponding and convergent opposition between enactment and text.

The *Second Introduction to the Wissenschaftslehre* (1798) insists that the character of the enactment is what fundamentally distinguishes the *Wissenschaftslehre*, what makes
its "entire structure and significance . . . utterly different
from those of the philosophical systems that have been cus-
tomary hitherto" (1:453). The contrast is a matter of origin,
of attentiveness to origin. Those philosophers whose systems
Fichte contrasts with the *Wissenschaftslehre* simply proceed
with various concepts, analyzing and combining them without considering whence they have derived these concepts.
Indifferent to the origin of the concepts, they produce philosophical systems that are simply products of their own
thought, artifacts. In the *Wissenschaftslehre*, by contrast, it is
a matter of returning to the origin of concepts, a matter of
bringing into play that self-relation, that "I am I," that is the
origin of origins. On the one hand, this origin is simply what
one is—or rather, what one could be said to be were the
origin not such as to exceed being and to withdraw from this
very saying, from all language (of being). As such, the
I—that is, that for which a pre-text would be woven around
the word "I"—is not so much to be observed, much less
manipulated, as rather enacted; it is indeed always already
enacted. On the other hand, a system can be produced only if
the enactment does not merely occur but is somehow com-
pounded in such a way as to be brought to show itself in
rigorous fashion. There must be a certain doubling of the
enactment, a formation of two different sequences of enact-
ments, that of the always already enacted I and that of the
philosopher, a contemplative enactment:

The *Wissenschaftslehre* is a very different matter. That which it
makes the object of its thought is not a dead concept that
would relate only passively to the investigation and from which
the investigation would make something only by its thought;
rather it is something living and active that produces knowledge from and through itself [*ein Lebendiges und Thätiges, das
aus sich selbst und durch sich selbst Erkenntnisse erzeugt*], and that
the philosopher merely contemplates [*zusieht*]. . . . But how
the object manifests itself is not his affair [*Sache*] but that of

the object itself, and he would be operating directly counter to his own aim if he did not leave it to itself but sought to intervene in the development of the appearance. [1:454]

The entire system of conceptual determination in the *Wissenschaftslehre* is aimed at allowing such a double enactment to come into play.

My concern here is merely to take note of this doubling.[5] For once reason undergoes displacement, once the I is redetermined in such a way as to render it capable of hovering, it will also be necessary to ask about the corresponding displacement of philosophy, to let a doubling come into play in this connection too, a doubling of the enactment of hovering, of enactment become hovering.

b | The *Wissenschaftslehre* is to present the Kantian system as a system; it is to constitute a systematic presentation of the system, to supply the systematic presentation lacking in Kant's text. Fichte stresses that the system is already present in Kant's text without, however, being presented there as such:

Now, I know very well that Kant by no means *set up* [*aufgestellt*] such a system. . . . However, I believe I also know with equal certainty that Kant *envisaged* [*sich . . . gedacht habe*] such a system; that everything that he actually propounds consists of fragments and consequences of this system, and that his assertions have sense and coherence only on this presupposition. [1:478]

Thus, in the *Wissenschaftslehre* it would be a matter neither of diverging from Kant nor even in a sense of completing his work but only of reforming his system into the presentation that as system it requires.

Preparation for the systematic presentation, including clarification of the sense of system and of presentation, is undertaken in Fichte's very remarkable text of 1794 "Ueber den Begriff der Wissenschaftslehre," the text that, even four years later, Fichte could describe as "the only writing up to now in which the philosophizing in the *Wissenschaftslehre* is itself taken up philosophically [*selbst philosophirt wird*] and that thus serves as an introduction to the system" (1:32). In this text he develops the concept of *Wissenschaftslehre* hypothetically, that is, leaving undecided whether a *Wissenschaftslehre* is possible and, in most respects, how it would be actually developed. He shows merely what its determination must be as a system; or, more precisely, he shows what its determination would be in abstraction from the actual development of the system and from the possible recoil of that development upon the system as such.

Fichte begins even prior to the question of system, begins with something on which it is said all would agree: philosophy is a science. What, then, is science? Fichte answers, again appealing to common agreement:

A science has systematic form; all propositions [*Sätze*] in it are connected in a single fundamental principle [*Grundsatz*] and in it are unified into a whole—this too one commonly admits. [1:38]

For science (*Wissenschaft*) the appropriate systematic form can only be one in the order of knowledge (*Wissen*). It is required that the fundamental principle be known with certainty and that it impart its certainty to all other propositions belonging to the system, which are thus themselves known with certainty by virtue of their connection with the fundamental principle. Within a science there are, then, two things that cannot be proved, that are rather presupposed for the very possibility of proof within that science: (1) the fundamental principle, which must already be established as certain prior to the science, and (2) the form of connection with the fundamental principle by which other propositions are imparted their certainty.

The concept of science thus outlined is not only formal but also quite classical. One can hardly help noting how vigorously Fichte underlines the function of unity. For example:

Every science must have a fundamental principle; of course it could, in accord with its inner character, consist entirely of a single, self-certain proposition [*an sich gewissen Satz*]—which, however, could then certainly not be called a fundamental principle [*Grundsatz*], since the proposition would not ground [*begrundete*] anything. However, it can also not have more than one fundamental principle, since in that case it would constitute not one but several sciences. [1:41–42]

Unity of principle is necessary: a science can contain only *one* fundamental principle, and multiple principles could only produce multiple sciences. Such unity is even in a sense sufficient: the inner character of science is such that there could be a science consisting of only one proposition, a proposition that would ground no others so as to be their *Grundsatz*, a science that would be no system at all.

Fichte makes explicit the corollary to the possibility of such a nonsystematic science. Systematic form, the form of connection between the fundamental principle and all other propositions, does not belong to the innermost essence of science; it is not "the goal of science" but only a "means of achieving the goal" in those cases in which the science would consist of several propositions—"not the essence of science but rather an accidental feature thereof" (1:42).

What might be such a nonsystematic science, such a science composed entirely of a single proposition? Fichte gives no indication, no example. Indeed, one cannot but wonder whether it would be possible even to imagine an example. Could there be a proposition from which no other would derive? Could there be a proposition (*Satz*) so hermetic as to ground no other proposition? Or would one need, rather, to forgo searching for an example among linguistic *Sätze*? Would one need perhaps to think of a movement, a leap, of another sort, of a sort that could be only enacted—a leap completely self-enclosed, absolved from all others, an absolute leap.

But Fichte gives no indication, no example. Instead he introduces a metaphorics, developing it in such a way as, in a sense, to inhibit any search for an example of nonsystematic, that is, absolute, science (as if this very concept were not of itself already sufficiently inhibiting). The metaphorics, which he introduces explicitly *as* a metaphorics, corresponds globally to the classical Kantian formulation of the metaphorics of edifice and ground (cf. A 319/B 375–76)—but now developed in quite a different way:

> Science would be an edifice; the principal purpose of this edifice would be stability [*Festigkeit*]. The ground is stable [firm (*fest*)], and insofar as the ground is laid out the purpose would be achieved. But because one cannot dwell on mere ground, because by it alone one cannot protect oneself either against intentional assault by enemy or against the unintended assaults of the weather, one erects on it walls, and above these a roof. All parts of the edifice are joined to the ground and to each other, and in this way the whole comes to be stable . . . ; and it is stable insofar as all of its parts rest on stable [firm (*fest*)] ground. [1:42]

Under certain unidentified conditions, the ground alone, though grounding nothing, would suffice for stability; one would be planted upon a self-sufficient earth, absolute science unperturbed from without. Or rather, the ground alone would suffice were there not conditions, were there not would-be intrusions from without, the assault of the enemy and of the elements. Upon the firm but exposed ground one must, then, erect a shelter in order to protect oneself from the assaults, a house that would supplement the security of ground by being erected securely upon that ground, borrowing its security, its stability, from that firm ground. Everything depends, then, on this transaction, on this double transfer of security.

A very classical order of grounding is thus brought into play and at the same time set in play also against itself by the insufficiency of ground. In classical terms it would be a matter of an ordered regression to ground, a regression by which would be attested the firmness of the ground (its appropriateness to serve as ground) and of the adjunction of the edifice to the ground. It would be a matter of regression that would exhibit the grounded as properly set back upon its ground.

Such a regression to ground is, in its simplest form, generated by the dynamics of the classical concept of science outlined by Fichte. Within a science every proposition (*Satz*) is to be grounded upon the fundamental principle (*Grundsatz*); the fundamental principle is to impart to each its certainty, that is, its stability as an item of knowledge. But since neither the fundamental principle nor its form of connection with other propositions can be proved within a science in the simplest classical sense, an extension of the regression is required, a further regression to a science of science in which would be proved the fundamental principles and the systematic forms of all (other) sciences. Such a science of science, identified with what previously has been called philosophy, Fichte renames: *Wissenschaftslehre*.

Within the science of science the dynamics of the classical concepts of science continues to operate, generating a regression to the fundamental principles of this fundamental science. This principle, as fundamental, can likewise not be proved in the simple regressive manner appropriate to other propositions in the *Wissenschaftslehre*. Nor can it be proved in the manner appropriate to the fundamental principles of all other sciences, namely, by transgressing the limits of the science toward a more fundamental science. The fundamental principle of the *Wissenschaftslehre* "is therefore utterly incapable of proof" (1:47); and its certainty must, accordingly, be immediate. It must be certain in and through itself, a proposition whose form and content are absolutely inseparable. The *Wissenschaftslehre* must also have systematic form, not simply because it is a science, for Fichte has granted the possibility of a nonsystematic science consisting of only one *Satz*, but because, in order that it ground, hence to that extent contain, the fundamental principles of all other sciences, it must be a science consisting of several *Sätze*. The determination of its form cannot come from without; the *Wissenschaftslehre* must have this form in itself, must ground it through itself. One could state the case even more strongly: since this form is presupposed for the very unfolding of the *Wissenschaftslehre* from the fundamental principle, it must be essentially grounded in the latter.

The *Wissenschaftslehre* would, then, extend the regression to ground in precisely such a way as to terminate it, to bring it to completion in a self-certain fundamental principle in which would be essentially gathered the multiplicity of propositions that could in a subsequent progression expand into the *Wissenschaftslehre* and in a further progression generate the multiplicity of sciences. It would seem that the utterly classical schema of regression/progression oriented by the simple opposition one/many is wholly intact. Philosophy would begin with the regressive turn back to the one fundamental principle and would in a sense consist of nothing but the elaboration of that turn.

And yet, at precisely the point where this schema would seem to be secured, Fichte abruptly introduces multiplicity, pluralizes the grounding unity; and though of course the pluralizing is, in accord with the character of "Ueber den Begriff der Wissenschaftslehre," only hypothetical, the entire actual *Wissenschaftslehre* will itself serve to confirm the hypothesis. Fichte broaches the pluralizing thus:

If beyond [*ausser*] the absolutely first fundamental principle there should be several fundamental principles of the *Wissenschaftslehre*, which would have to be only in part absolute, in part, however, conditioned by the first and highest [fundamental principle], since otherwise there would not be a single fundamental principle. . . . [1:49]

Fichte has insisted (1:42) and now repeats that there can be only one fundamental principle in a science; the *Wissenschaftslehre* must have a single (*einzig*) fundamental principle. And yet, the pluralizing move is explicit. Fichte's text betrays certain strategies by which the move to plurality would be limited or relativized: what would be the *single* fundamental principle is now designated as "der absolut-erste Grundsatz," and in a marginal note the other fundamental principles are said to be "im ersten Falle nicht Grund-, sondern abgeleitete Sätze" (1:49). Since these other fundamental principles would necessarily be conditioned either in form or in content by the absolutely first fundamental principle, there is mention of mediate determination of the other constituent—for example, form absolutely determined and hence content, as content of that form, mediately determined (1:50). But the pluralizing of ground cannot be so easily reinscribed in the order of progression, for in the other fundamental principles there remains something absolute, something not controlled by the absolutely first fundamental principle—as indeed Fichte finally acknowledges: there is "something absolute in them" (1:79). These other fundamental principles cannot be rendered merely intermediate and reintegrated into the classical order.

What, then, is the relation if not one of simple reintegration? How does the pluralizing of ground bear on the classical order of grounding? Can the pluralizing be regarded as somehow fulfilling the drive to ground, despite the classical identification of the latter with the drive to unity? Can the drive to ground culminate in a dispersion of ground, even of such limited extent, without all its governing oppositions being displaced? Or is the dispersion to be regarded as diverting the drive to ground, as opening up a space in which the regression constitutive of metaphysics would be diverted into a transgression of metaphysics, as releasing a spacing?

Fichte sketches two cases in which there would be no system, cases of pluralizing that would be utterly in opposition to the order of grounding. The first case is one of unlimited deferral, one in which there is nothing immediately certain:

We build our dwelling on the earth, the latter rests on an elephant, the latter on a turtle, the latter—on who knows what, and so on ad infinitum. [1:52]

The second case pluralizes horizontally rather than vertically. Reproducing the form of the Kantian antinomies, it opposes to the infinity of the first case a finite series, or rather a plurality of finite series. Each series would terminate in a self-grounding fundamental principle; and these various fundamental principles would have no connection among themselves, would be wholly isolated. It is as though "a number of threads ran through our spirit without being connected at any point" (1:53), without its being possible to connect them at any point by regression to a single grounding science. In this case there could be no *Wissenschaftslehre* but only the situation for which Fichte, again bringing the same metaphorics into play, offers the following image:

> Then our dwelling would certainly stand securely [*fest*], but instead of being a unified connected edifice it would be an aggregate of chambers, from none of which we could pass into the others; it would be a dwelling in which we would always lose our way and never come to be at home. There would be no light in it, and we would remain poor despite our riches, for the latter we could never estimate, could never regard as a whole, and never could know what we really possessed. . . . [1:53]

To both these cases Fichte opposes that in which there would be a complete and unitary system. He poses the opposition in a way that almost suppresses the very pluralizing that has come to be at issue, appealing now solely to the absolutely first fundamental principle and sketching the progression from it as follows:

> From it our knowledge spreads out in ever so many series, from each of which again proceed series, etc.; hence all must be securely connected in a single ring, which is attached to nothing but rather secures itself and the whole system by its own force. [1:54]

This ring is the earth, and the absolutely first fundamental principle its center. And so, again the metaphorics of ground and edifice comes into play, now in what would be a true image, an image of the truth of the human spirit:

> We have now a terrestrial globe [*Erdball*] that secures itself by its own force of gravity, a globe whose center point attracts all powerfully everything that we have erected, actually only on its

circumference and not in the air or obliquely; and that allows
not the slightest particle to escape from its sphere. [1:54]

A self-securing, self-delimiting sphere, well-rounded
truth—an ancient image, rendered post-Copernican, to
which now is added only the secure habitation that man
builds for himself upon the surface.

The question is whether such utter security is necessary in
order for there to be a system, whether the only alternative to
such absolutely centered truth would be unlimited dispersion such as Fichte has outlined in both vertical and horizon-
tal directions. The question is whether there can be a pluralizing of ground that is not simply unlimited and whether
such a pluralizing can be brought to supplement rather than
simply negate the classical order of grounding. Can the
pluralizing of ground perhaps displace and thereby reconstitute the order of grounding? Or is the very concept of ground
unhinged as soon as it is pluralized? Can the earth be decentered ever so slightly without veering off into the abyss? Is it
not already decentered ever so slightly by those habitations
that man has built for himself on its circumference?

Within the text "Ueber den Begriff der Wissenschaftslehre" ("the only writing . . . in which the philosophizing
in the *Wissenschaftslehre* is itself taken up philosophically")
the question of such (de)centeredness is developed through
the exposure of certain circles pertaining to the project of the
Wissenschaftslehre, specifically, four circlings into which the
human spirit is drawn in connection with that project. The
exposure occurs in the course of a progressively more fundamental elucidation of the sense of *system*.

In order that science be a system, it is required not only
that it have systematic form linking propositions to the
fundamental principle but also that it be complete, that it
contain all propositions to which the fundamental principle
can lead, that it be such that no further propositions can be
deduced. Positive proof of such completeness can occur only
if the fundamental principle, from which the progression has
been made, proves also to be the final result, for in this case

any further progression would simply retrace the same path. Hence, it is required that one recover the center at the very periphery of the sphere. Or rather, there belongs to the *Wissenschaftslehre* a circling back to the fundamental principle in such a way as would confound the opposition between regression and progression.[6]

And yet, Fichte adds, even if the fundamental principle is demonstrably exhausted and a complete system thus set up, it still does not follow that human knowledge as such is thereby exhausted. The hypothetical surplus thus posed serves to open a distinction that will come more and more to dominate this text; and it serves to introduce into the philosophizing in the *Wissenschaftslehre* a second circling. The distinction separates the fundamental sense of *system* from another with which, even in Fichte's text thus far, it has tended to coalesce:

> But insofar as it is simply science, a knowledge, in the formal sense, it is science of *something*; it has an object, and . . . it is clear that this object can be nothing but the system of human knowledge as such. [1:57]

It is a matter of distinguishing between the system of human knowledge, that is, the system intrinsic to the human spirit, and the presentation (*Darstellung*) of that system, that is, the "system" of propositions; and it is a matter of insisting that the former is the fundamental sense. The point is, then, that even if a presentation is complete there is no guarantee that what it presents is exhaustive of the human spirit, no guarantee that the "system" of human knowledge that it presents exhausts the system of human knowledge as such. This lack of guarantee, this insecurity, constitutes the second of the circles. Even if X is established as the fundamental principle of a demonstrably complete "system" (i.e., presentation) and even if within that "system" it is proven that there is only one system in human knowledge, one would still have to contend with the possibility that there might be in human knowledge another system too, a system whose presentation would involve a different fundamental principle, a "system" that might (or, more precisely, would have to) contradict thoroughly the first "system." Or rather, in a sense one could not contend with this possibility, could never deduce the impossibility of such an additional fundamental principle as would ground an additional "system." The deductively irreducible difference between system and presentation is what draws philosophy into a circle: if it is established that X is the fundamental principle of human knowledge as such (and not merely of the presentation of that system), then it follows that there is a single system in human knowledge (since this follows from X); but, on the other hand, it could be established that X, which grounds a single system, is the fundamental principle of human knowledge only by establishing that in human knowledge as such (and not merely in the presentation of it) there is precisely such a systematic configuration as is grounded by X, namely, a single system. Fichte concludes: "Thus there is here a circle from which the human spirit can never escape" (1:61). And yet, he adds: "One has no reason to be disconcerted by this circle." Because: "To wish that it be removed means to wish that human knowledge be completely groundless, that there be nothing whatsoever absolutely certain . . ." (1:62). One is not to be disconcerted by the circle, because that deductive circling can be centered precisely by a point of absolute certainty, by an act of the human spirit that would enact what is presented in such a way as to reduce the difference between spirit and presentation. Whatever decentering this second of the circlings produces in the presentation, in the text of the *Wissenschaftslehre*, would be compensated for by a recentering through enactment.

The third of the circles is even more explicitly drawn across the distinction between system and presentation, and its introduction is prepared by an elaboration of that distinction. Fichte begins with a rigorous restatement:

The object of the *Wissenschaftslehre* is after all the system of human knowledge. The latter subsists [*ist . . . vorhanden*] independently of the science of it; but through that science it is set up in systematic form. [1:70]

He then proceeds to sketch the most global features of each side, still, presumably, in a hypothetical, or rather now anticipatory, manner. That which on the side of the human spirit is independent of the science can be designated as actions (*Handlungen*); these constitute the content and their interrelations the form that belong originally to the human spirit, prior to the knowledge or science of it. In order that there be also a presentation or science of these actions or, rather, of the necessary actions of intelligence (Fichte narrowing the field still further, still, presumably, in an anticipatory manner), there is required a free action:

Now, by this free action something that is already in itself form, the necessary action of intelligence, is taken up as content into a new form, the form of knowledge or of consciousness; and accordingly the former action is an action of reflection. Those necessary actions are separated from the series in which they may occur in themselves and set up purely without any mixing; hence that action is also an action of abstraction. [1:72]

This abstracting reflection traces the third of the circles, traces it in the effort to draw the necessary actions of intelligence up into a new form, into the form of knowledge, of presentation. It is a very classical circle, the circle to which any inquiry, requiring foresight of what it would discover, is subject, the circle whose history is at least coextensive with the history of metaphysics. The circle is adapted now to the governing distinction between system and presentation, or, in more specific form, between the necessary actions of the intellect (in itself) and the abstracting reflection that would constitute its presentation:

If the necessary ways of action of intelligence in itself are to be taken up into the form of consciousness, they would have to be known already as such, hence they would have to be taken up already into this form; and we would be enclosed in a circle. [1:72]

The circle is equally in force if one focuses on the abstractive aspect of the presentative action: one can separate the necessary actions from those that are merely accidental, only if the line of this distinction is already drawn, only if the separation, the abstracting, has already taken place. There are no absolute rules for the abstracting reflection, no rules by which it could be carried out without foresight, that is, without entering into the circle.

Fichte suggests that this circularity is confirmed by the history of philosophy, confirmed in the sense of making the general character of that history intelligible, providing the genuine ground for the fact that what lies open in every human spirit comes to be clearly grasped and presented only after long wanderings in search of it. In strategic terms the circularity provides a schema by which can be granted the wanderings of the history of philosophy, the errors, the ruins left behind, *without* granting any essential closedness or concealment in the human spirit. It provides a schema by which to explain how it is that insight into oneself, self-knowledge, is progressive and not immediate, a progressive circling that cannot but come, as a whole at least, ever "closer to its goal" (1:74). It should not be overlooked, however, that this explanation itself moves in a circle, presupposing that the history of philosophy is essentially progressive and that the human spirit is essentially open to itself, fully self-present.

The fourth of the circles is generated by transposing the classical circle to the procedural order:

But the laws of reflection, which in the course of the science we find to be the only possible ones by which a *Wissenschafts-lehre* could be erected—even if they agree with those that we hypothetically presuppose as rules of our procedure—are still themselves the result of their prior application; and thus there is uncovered here a new circle: we have presupposed certain laws of reflection and now in the course of the science find these same laws to be the only correct ones. [1:74]

One ought, then, in view of this circle to forgo all claims to infallibility, claiming for the *Wissenschaftslehre* only probability. On the other hand, Fichte insists, "The system of the human spirit, whose presentation the *Wissenschaftslehre* is to be, is absolutely certain and infallible" (1:76); thus if men err, the source lies not in necessity but in the capacity of human judgment to confuse one law with another.

One ought to be astonished by this claim, this strategy by which all untruth, all play of dissimulation, all concealment, would be driven from the human spirit, exiled in mere errors of judgment. One ought to be astonished by the claim that the human spirit is essentially a pure space of truth, sheer unclouded transparency.[7] One ought to be astonished that this claim is accompanied by not the slightest admission of probability.

The claim allows Fichte to insist that it will always be a question only of whether the presentation that man constructs is accordant with the true system within the human spirit. Set thus aside, the philosopher would adopt the confession: "We are not lawgivers of the human spirit but rather its historiographers, . . . writers of pragmatic history" (1:77). Set thus aside from well-rounded truth, banished to its periphery, the philosopher would have only to construct his edifice in such a way as to utilize to the utmost the security that the firm surface of the earth would provide.

c | The *Wissenschaftslehre* is, then, to involve reflection in a double sense: first, in the sense that the system in the human spirit is to be reflected at the level of consciousness or knowledge, cast upon that level as in an image; second, in the sense that one is to attend to oneself, hence reflection in the sense of a turning, a bending, back upon oneself. Each moment of reflection is necessarily also one of abstracting, an abstracting of the necessary from the contingent and of self-consciousness from consciousness, respectively.[8] The intertwining of these two moments generates the fundamental structure of the *Wissenschaftslehre* as a reversion to self in which there is a doubling, a split between the observed I that can be made to show itself from itself and the observing I of the philosopher. The center of the structure, the bond that holds it together, is the enactment performed by the philosopher:

> This self-constructing I is no other than his own. He can intuit
> the aforementioned act of the I only in himself, and in order to
> be able to intuit it, he has to carry it out. . . . In this act
> [*Act*], I say, the philosopher contemplates himself, he intuits
> his act [*Handeln*] immediately, he knows what he does, because
> *he—does it.* [1:459–61]

It is a matter of a knowing that is irreducible to a saying, that can be captured by no text, a knowing that is sheer deed, a knowing by doing, enactment.

The double reflection is to be fundamental. It is to occur as a grounding reflection, as a reflection by which the regression to ground would be carried out. Thus, it is directed not simply at the representations (*Vorstellungen*) that are discovered when one turns back upon oneself, nor simply at those representations that are accompanied by a feeling of necessity, nor even simply at the systematic totality of such representations, which constitutes what is called experience (*Erfahrung*). The reflection is directed rather at the ground of experience; and as a reversion to self it is directed toward showing that and how the I is the ground of experience.

Thus, the *Wissenschaftslehre* begins by proposing this ground; that is, the first fundamental principle—the one to be designated as absolutely first, in contrast to the others—is a statement of what the I is, of the concept of the I. Fichte himself provides the commentary to this statement, provides it retrospectively in the two *Introductions* of 1798.[9]

However improper, however vigorously one might later need to retract it or cross it out, the question needs nevertheless to be posed if only in order that its impropriety can appear—the question: What is the I? Fichte's answer—an introductory and not systematic answer, to that extent improper, in need of being rewritten within the "system"—his answer is: It is a deed (*Thun*), an act (*Handeln*), and absolutely nothing more (1:440).

This means, in the first place, that by its very nature the I is active, not passive. It is not passive precisely because it is the final ground, preceded thus by nothing that could account for passivity in it; its very nature prohibits it from being dependent on something else capable of acting upon it and of thereby rendering it passive, dependent, grounded rather than ground. This absolutely active character of the I will prove to determine the system of syntheses, though in a way not entirely predictable; for, most remarkably, it will turn out that the I *does* contain passivity, even though by its very nature it cannot. The system of syntheses will be required in order to mediate between the terms of this contradiction; the critical question will be whether such mediation is bought at the price of decentering the I, letting it slip away from its very nature, its true essence, its "what."

That the I is act means, second, that it is distinct from being, that it has no being proper, that it is not *something* that is active, not an active being. It is not as though there were something in which activity would inhere, a being in itself to which activity would then be added as an inherent character, something that would first be and then act. One would need again to say: the I is act and absolutely nothing more. One would need to say it more explicitly: the I is act and absolutely nothing more, not even being. And one would need then to be attentive to the recoil of the said upon the saying, crossing out the "is," writing it under erasure. One would need to write: the I ̶i̶s̶ beyond being—thereby contesting while also confirming what Fichte says about the word "being," that without it "no language would be possible" (8:320).

Of course, one cannot simply overlook the way in which Fichte tends to set up the opposition between act and being, for example, in the following passage from the *Second Introduction*:

Let me take this opportunity to say once with full clarity: the essence of transcendental idealism and of the presentation in the *Wissenschaftslehre* in particular consists in its regarding the concept of being as by no means a *first* and original concept but merely as derivative, as a concept derived specifically through opposition to activity, and hence as a merely *negative* concept. [1:498–99]

One could hardly compose a more classical statement of metaphysical opposition, a statement that would more perfectly exemplify the oppositional hierarchism constitutive of metaphysics. The statement accordingly betrays the extent to which Fichte's move beyond being merely repeats, at a level proposed as more fundamental, the classical gesture, the metaphysical turn from beings to being. The question, an ancient question, is whether this repetition might also divert the classical move, setting it adrift, turning metaphysical regression into transgression ἐπέκεινα τῆς οὐσίας.

How is the I as act to be specified? How is the act to be characterized? Or taking the question from Fichte himself and for a moment passing over its impropriety: "How is the I for itself? [*wie ist das Ich für sich selbst?*]" (1:458). What is the form that its being would take if it were not beyond being? What species of act would it exemplify if act were not even less susceptible than being (and for the same reason) to being regarded as a genus divisible into species? Fichte answers with an imperative:

Think of yourself, construct the concept of yourself; and notice how you do it. [1:458]

How does one do it? By reflecting, becoming an object to oneself. It is a matter of a self-reverting activity (*in sich zurückkehrendes Handeln*), a turning back upon oneself in such a manner that in the act there is immediate identity of subject and object. Such is the way that the I presents itself to itself; such would be the way the I *is* for itself, its being for itself, were it not beyond being.

Here one would need almost constantly to include a reminder of the conditional, to mark the impropriety of the language (of being).

The I's being-for-itself is not to be contrasted with what the I is in itself. It is not as though the I would first *be*, as a

being-in-itself, a thing-in-itself, and would then turn back
upon itself. It *is*—or more properly would be—the activity
of turning back upon itself and absolutely nothing more. If it
were being, the I would be simply, absolutely self-reverting
activity:

> That act is simply the concept of the I, and the concept of the
> I is the concept of that act; both are exactly the same. . . . I
> and self-reverting act are fully identical concepts. [1:460, 462]

The I, self-reverting act, is to be shown to be the ground
of experience, specifically of those representations that are
accompanied by a feeling of necessity and that are taken to be
representations of objects external to the I. And yet, Fichte
also insists that it is to be shown "that this act would be
impossible without another, whereby there arises for the I a
being outside itself" (1:458). Self-reverting act, the well-
centered I, would be the condition for the appearance of
external objects; *but also*, even if in a sense that can perhaps be
differentiated, the appearance of external objects, of the
not-I, is the condition of the self-reverting I. In short, the I
conditions the not-I, and the not-I conditions the I. Though
Fichte would reorder the conditioning, insisting that the I is
ground and the not-I grounded (cf. 1:457–58), the syntheses
that constitute the critique of theoretical knowledge turn in
this circle, threatening from the outset to decenter the I.

This circle is not reducible to any of those four circles that
Fichte traces in "Ueber den Begriff der Wissenschaftslehre."
Rather than simply circling back to the grounding principle,
it is a circling also away from it, a circling that threatens
every self-completing return. And it threatens equally the
reduction of the circle generated by the distinction between
system and presentation, the recentering through enactment, threatens it by threatening to decenter that very
enactment. And compared to the classical circle of foresight
and to the circle that is its procedural correlate, the circle that
has now been broached is what one could call more radical,
were the radical, *radix*, root, not so thoroughly appropriated
to the very metaphorics of ground that this circle serves to

put in jeopardy; for it is a matter of self-precedence not simply in the order of knowledge but in that of being, or, more precisely, in an order that exceeds even being. The circle is, to risk an ancient figure, a circle of difference, more so than any of the four. It is a circle that threatens the centeredness of the perfect sphere, well-rounded truth, as well as the series of securities that would protect pure self-reversion from every incursion of alterity. It is a circle whose threat cannot be easily isolated and contained, for it is reproduced, its image redrawn, at so many levels of Fichte's (pre)text—redrawn, for example, in the image of the supplementary edifice that would be erected on the exposed ground, borrowing its security in a transaction that would amount to a double transfer of security; or, again, in the problem of the pluralizing of ground, of the pluralizing that would neither simply negate nor be reintegrated into the classical order of grounding.

d   The first fundamental principle of the *Wissenschlaftslehre* simply expresses the concept of the I, expresses it in a way that, with utter appropriateness, withdraws it from being:

> Originally the I posits absolutely its own being [*Das Ich setzt ursprünglich schlechthin sein eigenes Sein*]. [1:98]

Fichte is explicit about the Kantian affiliation:

> In his deduction of the categories Kant pointed to our proposition as the absolutely fundamental principle of all knowledge; but he never definitively set it up *as* fundamental principle. [1:99]

Fichte presents the principle as issuing from an abstracting reflection that in a sense repeats the most fundamental phase of Kant's deduction of the categories, namely, the regression expressed in Kant's insistence that "it must be possible for the 'I think' to accompany all my representations" (B 131). In very briefest outline, the Fichtean repetition involves beginning with a proposition that is admitted to be perfectly certain, namely, the law of identity, "A = A," of proceeding from that proposition to what it presupposes, namely, the assertion "I am I," that is, the assertion of the identity of the I. And then it is a matter of grasping that this identity is not just a fact but rather an act, the self-reverting, self-positing act that the I could be said to be if it were not beyond being. And it is a matter of expressing this act in the first—the absolutely first—fundamental principle.[10]

A similar abstracting reflection leads to the second fundamental principle. In this case it is a matter of beginning with the absolute assertion of the principle of opposition, "~A ≠ A," in which is expressed a positing of ~A in its opposition to A, the counterpositing that is materially conditioned (by the positing of A) but is in form original. It is a matter then of proceeding to the fundamental condition presupposed by this assertion, namely, the form of opposition as such, absolute opposition, which can only be opposition to what is absolutely posited, to the I, whose absolute positing is expressed in the first fundamental principle. Hence:

Nothing is originally posited except the I; and this alone is absolutely [schlechthin] posited. . . . Hence there can be an absolute opposition only to the I. But that which is opposed to the I = not-I. [1:104]

This opposition is what is expressed in the second fundamental principle: a not-I is opposed absolutely to the I.

Both abstracting reflections thus carry out a regression back to a dimension that one might call transcendental, the dimension whose operation is presupposed by all experience. The first fundamental principle expresses the originary identity of that dimension, the second fundamental principle the originary difference within it. And yet, both the position (identity) and the opposition (difference) are absolute (even if only in form, as in the case of opposition). How is this possible? How can there be absolute identity that nevertheless admits difference, even absolute difference? How can what would be the dimension of ground admit such difference without violating its very nature, without itself being decentered by the incursion of alterity? The circle has again been broached, the fifth circle, irreducible to those four that Fichte so openly grants.

This circle is retraced throughout the *Wissenschaftslehre*, retraced in the sense not of mere repetition but of being redrawn so as to be opened or closed, widened or narrowed. These retracings and the way in which they structure the *Wissenschaftslehre* can be gathered most easily from certain passages in which Fichte allows his discourse to open upon the whole.

The first such opening upon the whole occurs in the introduction of the third fundamental principle, for which there remains only the alternative of being absolute in content, conditioned in form. Fichte outlines in very broad terms the sense in which it is conditioned in form and absolute in content:

The *task* that it poses *for action* is determinately given by the two preceding propositions, but not the resolution of the same. The latter occurs unconditionally and absolutely by a decree of reason [*Machtspruch der Vernunft*]. [1:105–6]

The form of the third fundamental principle is conditioned by the other two fundamental principles in the sense that they determine the task expressed in it, while leaving undetermined the accomplishment of that task, leaving it to an absolute decree. Fichte continues:

We begin, therefore, with a deduction and proceed with it as far as we can. The impossibility of carrying it further will undoubtedly show us the point at which we have to break off and appeal to that unconditioned decree of reason that will emerge from the task. [1:106]

This passage divides the course of the *Wissenschaftslehre* into three stages.

First: "We begin, therefore, with a deduction. . . ." The beginning opens the circle by letting the opposition between the first and the second fundamental principles come into play—the opposition between position and opposition, hence not just an instance of opposition but opposition as such. It is a matter of opposition between the positings expressed in the first two fundamental principles, the opposition between the self-positing I and the positing of the not-I; such is the locus of opposition as such. If the I as such absolutely posits itself and neither posits nor is posited by anything else, then how can there be a not-I counterposited over against it? Each side would, it seems, simply eliminate the other, not just through logical contradiction but, more significantly, through the way in which the essential alterity of the not-I would violate self-sufficient interiority, the pure self-relation, which the I as such would be. The task, then, is one of *synthesis*, of narrowing and eventually closing the circle that has been opened between the first and the second fundamental principle; the task is that of a synthesis by which the I would be joined to the not-I without mutual elimination. The third fundamental principle is the expression of this task and of the manner in which it would be accomplished, namely, by mutual limitation; the synthesis must be of such a character that the opposed terms, the I and the not-I, come to limit one another, each eliminating the reality of the other but only in part. In turn, such limitation is possible only if the terms have parts, can be partitioned, that is, are divisible—hence, the third fundamental principle: "In the I, I oppose a divisible not-I to the divisible I" (1:110). Such a synthesis would allow the opposites to remain without mutual elimination: The not-I would be what the (limited) I is not, each being posited to the extent that (in the same measure as) the other is not posited. And yet, in this formulation there is a compounding of the task, and the circle that would at least be narrowed is opened and extended in another direction; for the limited I that the synthesis would join to the (limited) not-I is by its very limitation opposed to the absolute I expressed in the first fundamental principle. The circle between I and not-I is simply replaced by a circle between the limited I and the absolute I, between finite and infinite. The synthesis, the deduction that is to carry it through, must attend to both oppositions, to both circles.

Second: "We begin, therefore, with a deduction and proceed with it as far as we can." How does the deduction proceed? It is a matter at each step of seeking out the oppositions that remain and of uniting them through a new ground, a conjunction, of further synthesis. Thus reiterating the move from antithesis to synthesis to new antithesis, the deduction will, step by step, narrow the circle. As the circle narrows, it converges on a center—not, however, on the original center expressed in the first fundamental principle, the self-positing I, the center of well-rounded truth. Most remarkably, it converges rather on *imagination,* while the original center proves to have been displaced. The ground, the absolute ground, proves to have shifted.

And yet, third, the convergence is incomplete: "The impossibility of carrying it further will undoubtedly show us the point at which we have to break off. . . ." The circle is narrowed but not closed, and it is necessary finally to "appeal to that unconditioned decree of reason that will emerge from the task." This transition would abruptly shift the center back to reason become practical, would recenter everything in the first fundamental principle, whose genuine significance would become manifest only at this final stage.

A second opening upon the whole occurs in a two-part passage belonging to a Note (*Anmerkung*) that Fichte inserts at a major juncture in the deduction. The passage begins by opening the circle: since the I, closed within itself, can neither act upon nor be acted upon by the not-I directly, what is required is mediation by which some indirect transaction would become possible:

The genuine highest task that embraces all others is: how can the I have a direct effect on the not-I, or the not-I on the I, since both are to be utterly opposed to each other. One interposes some X in between them, on which both may act, so that they also work indirectly upon one another. But one soon discovers that there must again be some point in this X at which I and not-I directly meet. To prevent this, one interposes between them and replaces the sharp boundary by a new term Y. But it soon appears that here too, as in X, there must be a point at which the two opponents directly touch one another. And so it would go on ad infinitum, if the knot were not cut, rather than loosed, by an absolute decree [*Machtspruch*] of reason, which the philosopher does not make but merely exhibits: since there is no way of unifying the not-I with the I, *let there be* no not-I at all. [1:143–44]

The mediation must be reiterated, the synthesis extended in such a way as to narrow the circle. It would have to be reiterated ad infinitum, were the knot not cut and another infinity exhibited, allowed to proclaim itself, to proclaim the demand, the categorical demand: let there be no not-I at all. Let everything be brought under the I, brought into accord with the I as though it were posited by the I.

The matter can be regarded from another side, for the synthesis that would narrow the circle between I and not-I would by that very move open up and widen a circle between the absolute (self-positing) I and the limited I (opposed to a not-I). This circle too would need to be narrowed; there would be need for a synthesis of finite and infinite. The second part of the passage is addressed to this need:

One can regard the matter still from another side.—Insofar as the I is limited by the not-I, it is finite; in itself, however, as posited through its own absolute activity, it is infinite. These two, its infinity and its finitude, are to be unified. But such a unification is in itself impossible. For a time, indeed, the conflict is settled by mediation; the infinite delimits the finite. But finally, once the utter impossibility of the attempted unification becomes manifest, finitude as such must be superseded [*aufgehoben*]; all limits must disappear, and the infinite I must alone remain, as one and as all. [1:144]

The transition is the same: from the failure of synthesis, its failure to close the circle, *to* the proclamation of an infinity by which the circle would be decisively closed, the proclamation of an infinity that *ought* to be, closure, the supersession of finitude, as a categorical imperative: "Our idealism is not dogmatic but practical, does not determine what *is* but what *ought* to be" (1:156).

Everything is recentered, and, in the end, the first fundamental principle proves to be absolutely first, the threat of plurality being decisively overcome in the transition from theoretical to practical. Only in this recentering shift back to the absolutely first fundamental principle does the genuine significance of that principle come to be determined. Thus, it is only after the shift, the transition to the practical, has been consolidated that the following determination is offered, a retrospective opening upon the whole, set appropriately in parentheses:

(Here the meaning of the principle, *the I posits itself absolutely,* first becomes wholly clear. Therein it is not a matter of talking about [*Es ist . . . nicht die Rede von*] the I given in actual consciousness; for the latter is never absolute, but its state always is grounded, either immediately or mediately, on something outside the I; it is a matter rather of talking about an idea of the I that must necessarily lie at the ground of its infinite practical demand, which, however, is unattainable for our consciousness and so can never appear immediately therein [though it may, of course, mediately, in philosophical reflection].) [1:277]

Also, from this retrospection, the significance of the initial theoretical act comes finally to be determined, the significance of setting up the absolutely first fundamental principle, the expression of the absolute I, at the beginning—*as* the beginning—of the *Wissenschaftslehre*. The genuine significance lies in the determination of that act as being ultimately not theoretical but practical, a response to the infinite practical demand, a matter of duty. Even more retrospectively—in the *Second Introduction*—Fichte explicitly calls the *Wissenschaftslehre* a product "of practical necessity." He continues:

Transcendental idealism thus appears at the same time as the only dutiful mode of thought in philosophy, as that mode of thought in which speculation and the moral law are most intimately united. I *ought* in my thinking to set out from the pure I, and to think of the latter as absolutely self-active; not as determined by things, but as determining them. [1:467]

Retrospectively, a prephilosophical condition proves to be required for philosophy, namely, a consciousness of duty or of freedom, a consciousness that can prove itself only in being enacted. At the end it can be said still more significantly: "What sort of philosophy one chooses depends, therefore, on what sort of man one is."

But let us withdraw—at least temporarily—from this end in which one would have circled back to the beginning and recentered everything. Let us withdraw—if only to be able to gauge the force of that recentering—to that stage prior to the practical decree, that stage where the system of syntheses narrows the circle, making it converge on a *displaced* center.

It was observed above that there are actually two dynamically interconnected circles, that is, two dimensions in which syntheses are to be deduced. The first is that of the opposition between the I and the not-I; the corresponding synthesis Fichte calls the synthesis of efficacy. The other dimension is that of the opposition between the absolute I and the limited I; the synthesis in this dimension he calls the synthesis of substantiality. In both dimensions the problem is ultimately the same. How can there be limitation in the I? How can the absolutely self-positing I be limited by something beyond itself, by a not-I? How can the I be an I and yet be subject to receptivity, that is, be passive, finite? How is a finite I possible? Or, in Fichte's precise formulation, how is it possible for the following principle—the principle of the theoretical *Wissenschaftslehre*—to hold: the I posits itself as limited by the not-I?

The two dimensions represent the two directions in which a resolution of this problem might be sought. In the first, that of the synthesis of efficacy, it might be supposed that the passivity of the I arises from an activity in the not-I, that the activity of the not-I *causes* affection in the I. In this case the I would be limited by the not-I, but it would not be aware of its limitation, would be merely passively acted upon, acted upon in a way totally at variance with its nature as an I. The I would be determined by the not-I but would not posit itself as so determined.

The dimension of substantiality would complement perfectly that of efficacy. Now it would be supposed that the I has the power, independently of any influence of the not-I, of positing passivity, limitation, in itself. But then, this limitation would have no relation to anything in the not-I as its cause. Thus, the I would posit itself as determined but not as determined by the not-I.

Hence, Fichte concludes:

> Thus both syntheses, employed in isolation, fail to explain what they should, and the contradiction complained of above still remains: if the I posits itself as determined, it is not determined by the not-I; if it is determined by the not-I, it does not posit itself as determined. [1:148]

Clearly, what is required is that the two syntheses not be employed in isolation. What is required is a synthesis of the syntheses.

The two alternatives of efficacy and substantiality, the resolutions they would generate, represent forms of realism and idealism. Realism, corresponding to the synthesis of efficacy, locates the ground of limitation in the not-I, thus taking account of the finite I's relation to the not-I, of its finitude in the sense of dependence on something external, *but not* of its nature as an I, as absolutely self-positing. On the other hand, idealism, corresponding to the synthesis of substantiality, locates the ground in the absolute I, thus taking account of the finite I's nature as an I, of its I-character (that it posits itself, is sheer self-reverting act), *but not* of its finitude. What is thus required is a synthesis of realism and idealism.

Let us, then, regard the system of syntheses as such a synthesis or convergence of realism and idealism. The system divides, then, into a series of stages. At each stage an idealism, which takes account of the I-character of the I, and a realism, which takes account of finitude, are exhibited in their opposition. The progression through the successive stages mediates the opposition, rendering the types of realism and idealism less one-sided, making the two sides converge.

The four most important stages of this progression can be indicated without entering further into the intricacies of this incomparably complex structure of determinations. At the first of these stages the opposition is between what Fichte calls dogmatic idealism and dogmatic realism. According to the former, the I is simply the cause of those presentations that constitute experience of objects; the not-I has no sort of reality apart from presentation.[11] The one-sidedness of this position is evident: it simply gives no account of how the I is limited. On the other hand, dogmatic realism (one form of which is Spinozism) stands at the opposite extreme: the not-I is simply regarded as the cause of presentation and, hence, as the real ground of everything. Clearly, this position involves the most extreme failure to account for the I-character of the I, for its character as self-positing. In the wake of such opposition, the outcome is, Fichte anticipates, that "all finite reason is thrown into conflict with itself and embroiled in a circle" (cf. 1:154–56). But this circling that belongs to finite reason has first to be exhibited in its full force.

At the second of the major stages the opposition is between what Fichte calls qualitative idealism and qualitative realism. According to the former, the not-I has no reality in itself. Nevertheless, in contrast to dogmatic idealism, this second form of idealism does not regard the not-I as having no sort of reality at all; rather, it is considered to have its proper reality but only as the result of a transference of reality to it by the I. In terms of activity and passivity, the activity in the not-I is simply a result of the I's positing of passivity in itself. The one-sidedness is evident: it is left unintelligible how the I could ever posit passivity in itself, for the I *as* I (as self-positing) posits only activity (reality) in itself. This position takes no account of any affection of the not-I on the I by which the I might be limited, might come to have passivity in itself. It takes insufficient account of finitude— even if the insufficiency is less than with the previous variety of idealism. On the other side stands qualitative realism, and according to this position the not-I is the ground of the passivity in the I; that is, qualitative realism regards the not-I as having independent reality and as operating on the I, as causing passivity in the I. The not-I is taken as a thing-in-itself. But here too there is one-sidedness: it is not explained how a thing-in-itself could operate on an I; since, considered in its I-character, the I is what it posits itself to be, it could be limited by such a not-I only if it posited itself as so limited. Qualitative realism fails to do justice to the I-character of the I—even if the failure is less radical than with the previous variety of realism (cf. 1:171–78).

The third of the stages is that of quantitative idealism and quantitative realism. For quantitative idealism the opposition between the I and the not-I is founded on a positing rather than existing prior to (independently of) all positing; in other words, this position contends that it is a law of the I to posit in such a way as to institute opposition between itself and a not-I, that is, in such a way as to institute finitude. This means, in effect, that the I simply posits itself as finite—that is, that it is absolutely finite. Thus, in contrast to the previous types of idealism, quantitative idealism takes some account of finitude. However, the way in which it is taken into account effectively abolishes it: this idealism simply attempts to incorporate finitude into the I-character of the I, to make it absolute. But "absolute finitude" is a contradiction. On the other side stands quantitative realism. Unlike the previous form of realism, this position does not assume that the not-I has independent reality; it does not suppose a thing-in-itself. Rather, it maintains merely that there is a real limitation present in the I without any contribution on the part of the I, that is, a limitation the ground of which does not lie in the I. This position is distinctive in that it holds back from the further inference to an independently existing not-I as the real cause of this limitation. Yet even this realism remains one-sided. It too fails to take sufficient account of the I-character of the I: it cannot explain how a *real* determination could become a determination *for* the I—that is, it cannot show how the I's absolute positing of itself could be determined by something extrinsic to that positing (cf. 1:181–90).

The final stage involves an idealism in which the position of quantitative idealism is further refined: the positing of the opposition between the I and the not-I is no longer regarded as an additional act attached, as it were, to the fundamental act of self-positing (which the I is), but rather these are considered one and the same act. But this advance beyond quantitative idealism only serves to pose in more subtle form the same problem: how can the I, which *is* simply the positing of itself, ever posit opposition to itself? Finitude remains still unaccountable. Over against this idealism stands a realism equally refined. In contrast to qualitative realism, this final realism does not maintain the existence of a not-I independent of the I. Nor, in contrast to quantitative realism, does it even suppose that there is present in the I a determination, a bound, not grounded in the I. Rather, it maintains merely that there occurs a check (*Anstoss*) to the I's activity (i.e., its positing of itself), a check that, instead of setting a definite bound to the I's activity, merely serves to give the I the task of setting bounds to itself, of determining itself. In order, then, to set these bounds, the I must oppose a not-I to itself, at the same time conjoining that not-I as object to itself as subject. Yet even this realism, refined though it be, shares the inadequacy that all realism has with respect to the I-character of the I: it explains the check— hence, the requirement that the I be determined—*as* something involving no contribution from the side of the I; but it leaves it entirely unintelligible how the check could ever be something *for* the I so as to perform its role (cf. 1:205–11).

Despite the convergence of realism and idealism, despite the narrowing of the circle, its convergence, opposition still remains; the circle remains open, final synthesis unattained. And yet, the synthesis must in some sense be possible, for otherwise the principle that expresses the synthesis could not hold; nor, then, could the other (fundamental) principles from which it is deduced. Thus, if there cannot be a synthesis

in the sense of a resolution or even dissolution of all opposition, there must be a synthesis of another kind, a synthesis
that would consist in holding together the opposed terms.
The interplay in which such a kind of synthesis would occur
Fichte calls the power of *imagination*:

This interplay of the I in and with itself, whereby it posits
itself at once as finite and infinite—an interplay that consists,
as it were, in self-conflict and is self-reproducing in that the I
endeavors to unify what is not unifiable, now attempting to
bring the infinite into the form of the finite, now, driven back,
positing it again outside the latter, and in that very moment
seeking once more to bring it into the form of finitude—this is
the power of imagination [*das Vermögen der Einbildungskraft*].
. . . The imagination posits no sort of fixed limits; for it has
itself no fixed standpoint; reason alone posits anything fixed, in
that it first gives fixity to imagination itself. Imagination is a
power that hovers [*schwebt*] in the middle between determination and nondetermination, between finite and infinite.
[1:215–16]

Imagination has no fixed standpoint but is the movement of
displacement as such; it posits no fixed limits but circulates
among the opposites so as to hold them together, its very
displacement delimiting a space of opposition. Imagination
hovers in between opposites so as to hold them together in
their opposition, so as to hold together the finite and the
infinite, so as to hold together relation to a not-I and absolute
self-positing. Imagination is the power of spacing those
oppositions that can be neither dissolved nor eliminated from
theoretical knowledge. Imagination is the spacing of truth.

The enactment of such spacing, this enactment of hovering that Fichte calls imagination, must be doubled at the
level of philosophy itself. The critical investigation of the
ground of theoretical knowledge must reflect on precisely
this oppositional space composed by imagination; and so,
this opposition, "something contradictory, . . . must be laid
at the ground of all our philosophizing" (1:283). At the level
of philosophical reflection the opposition appears in the guise

of the opposition between idealism and realism; thus Fichte says regarding these two courses:

One ought to follow neither of these courses: one ought to reflect neither on the one alone nor on the other alone but on both together, to hover in between the two opposed determinations of this idea. This is the business of the *creative* imagination [*schaffenden Einbildungskraft*] . . . . It is this power that determines whether one philosophizes with, or without, spirit. [1:284]

The theoretical *Wissenschaftslehre* converges on imagination, on this displaced center, this moving point, this hovering between opposites, this spacing of truth. And from what is thus disclosed, the philosophical reflection is reflected back to itself, disclosed to itself, as an enactment of creative imagination.

In the end the *Wissenschaftslehre* would subordinate this enactment of creative imagination to another, the enactment of freedom, of duty, the inward turn that would break absolutely with alterity and with sensibility, that would withdraw into what in classical terms one would call the intelligible (cf. 1:467) or, rather, would project such withdrawal as the infinite practical demand. The circle would be closed by having its closure projected as categorical imperative. The classical order of grounding would, in the end, be secured.

But suppose again that one withdraws from that end. Suppose that one insists on withdrawing from this quite classically metaphysical withdrawal. Suppose that one refuses the practical way back to the center, back to the security of ground. It goes without saying that the logic (I write the word under erasure) of such refusal would be exorbitant: there could be no question of grounding a refusal whose very function would be to inhibit the shift that would bring the classical order of grounding back into force. One might propose a discourse of provocation, as Socrates was provoked to engage in philosophy by the Delphic oracle, though the utmost care would be needed to delimit the conditions and prohibitions of such a discourse. And one might then bring to bear certain provocative experiences of moral ambiguity and of nonfreedom, or certain attestations of a bond with sense, as in art, to say nothing of the experience of technology, in which everything comes to be precisely—that is, actually, not just teleologically—as if posited by reason.

The displacement would then remain in force. Instead of being secured, in the end, as self-positing ground, the I would remain the interplay of and with opposites that Fichte calls imagination. Even if the hovering I cannot but interpose a substrate between those opposites that it holds together (cf. 1:224–25), conferring reality upon them, rendering them intuitable (cf. 1:226–27), drifting thus into the deception of being (cf. 1:224–25; 8:320), still this I would withdraw essentially from being. One would, then, need especially to gauge this withdrawal, to chart the way in which imagination could hold together the opposites without the (self-)deceptive drift into being, the way in which it could enact a spacing of truth beyond being.

The circle(s) of reason would, then, have been redrawn as the displaced circling of imagination, withdrawn from being and ground, drawn into the spacing of oppositions. Philosophy would end—or be denied an end—with imagination hovering ἐπέκεινα τῆς οὐσίας, hovering between heaven and earth, a dove.

3 | ENROUTINGS —

The Eccentricity of Reason

Reason ought, then, to be radical.

And yet, reason is not the *radix* but only a stem, one of two: "The common root of our power of knowledge divides and throws out two stems, one of which is *reason*" (A 835/B 863). To become utterly radical would mean, then, to usurp the place of the common root, to draw itself back to "the point at which the common root of our power of knowledge divides and throws out two stems, one of which is *reason*," reducing the space of the opposition to a point, displacing itself from that very spacing that would delimit it. In becoming utterly radical, reason would fulfill the ought, the ought as such and not just some particular duty; and yet, by displacing itself through the withdrawal toward the *radix*, reason would disrupt the very spacing in which the ought as such is constituted. As reason becomes unopposed, its imperative becomes assertoric, or, rather, the very distinction between imperative and assertion is reduced. Were reason to become utterly radical, it would withdraw the very imperative that would have commanded it to become such. Radical reason would master everything except the slippage, the erosion, of its own determining sense.

A corresponding semantic spacing can be traced across a certain field, can be traced by marking a certain way, a route, across that very rich, very complex field.[1] The route begins with itself, with its semantic double, with the *route* that reason would follow back to the common *root*, the *routing* by which it would steer itself back to that point at which it would become radical, would be fixed by the root, *enrooted*. *Route* stems from the Latin *rupta* (*broken*), from *rumpere* (*to break*), and thus displays its original, radical, sense: *division*,

67

detachment. The route of reason would be preeminently divisive, dividing reason against itself in that very movement that would restore unbroken unity, detaching reason from that very spacing by which its sense would be determined. *Route* is also *rout*, and among the senses into which the latter is spread there is the following:

Of swine: to turn up the soil with the snout in search of food;

and, manifestly akin to this, the following:

To root *out,* to extirpate.

Reason would take up its utmost, its ownmost duty only at the risk of also being cast in(to) the state of swine routing in the soil, turning it up, deforming it perhaps even more than do those blind subterranean creatures who, in Kant's word, fill it with their *Maulwurfsgänge.* And yet, *rout* both assembles and scatters the two moments, including in its semantic spread the following:

To assemble, to gather or herd *together*; also, to take part in a gathering;

To put (an army, body of troops, etc.) to rout; to compel to flee in disorder. To disperse, dispel, scatter, drive away.

Gathering and dispersing the moments *gathering* and *dispersing*, *rout* portrays the rout of reason en route to the common root.

The etymological complexity, which is considerable, would perhaps warrant letting the rout be portrayed also in the elusiveness of the common (etymological) root that would decisively unify and govern the field, the common, but to us unknown, root from which would issue the two stems *root* and *route*; or, more pointedly, *enrooting* and *en route*. Or one might just imagine such a common root, just imagine that the route of reason is semantically predetermined as the route back to the common root. One might just imagine, in the singular, putting orthography in service to imagination: *enrouting.*

a   The outbreak of metaphor that occurs near the end of the
Transcendental Analytic is without parallel elsewhere in the
Critique of Pure Reason. Almost openly it betrays that text and
through its betrayal offers an opening upon certain questions
that secretly govern that text while remaining systematically
suppressed therein. More closely considered, this outbreak of
metaphor is a double betrayal. Not only does it, like a
traitor, violate what its belonging to that text would require,
thus exposing the text to violence from without, but also it
reveals something about that text, something not manifest,
something that Kant himself almost certainly did not intend
the metaphorical outbreak to reveal, something that perhaps
he could not have intended it to reveal.

Through the first betrayal it opens upon the question of a
metaphorics of reason, broaches the question: How can a
metaphorics be operative within reason as such—and especially in reason's critical reflection on itself—without violating the very determination of reason as such, its determination in opposition to the other stem, sensibility? How can a
metaphorics of reason be operative without compromising
that opposition and risking the utter rout of reason? How can
reason admit a spacing in which it could mix with sense
without dissolving its opposition to sense? How is reason, in
its classical determination, to be displaced into such a space?

Through the other betrayal the outbreak opens upon the
question of the spacing of the text itself, the question of its
textuality. I shall begin with this second opening.

The metaphorical eruption to which I have referred is
quite strategically located. It divides the Transcendental
Analytic proper from the concluding summary account organized around the distinction between phenomena and
noumena—that is, its functions as the hinge on which the
concluding synthetic account turns. Thus placed, it also in
effect hinges the Transcendental Dialectic to the Transcendental Analytic. What erupts here into metaphor is one of
the primary articulations of the *Critique of Pure Reason*:

> We have now not only traveled across the land of pure un-
> derstanding and carefully surveyed every part of it but have

also measured its extent and determined the place of everything
in it. But this land is an island, enclosed by nature itself
within unalterable limits. It is the land of truth (an enchanting
name) surrounded by a wide and stormy ocean, the native
home of illusion, where many a fog bank and many a swiftly
melting iceberg give the deceptive appearance of farther shores,
deluding the adventurous seafarer ever anew with empty hopes
and engaging him in enterprises that he can never abandon and
yet is unable to bring to an end. But before we venture on this
sea, to explore it in all directions and to obtain assurance
whether there be any basis for such hopes, it will be useful still
to cast a glance at the map of the land that we are about to
leave. . . . [A 235–36/B 294–95).

This metaphorical hinge, connecting major segments of the
Critique of Pure Reason, serves also to attach the articulation
and movement of that text to another articulation, one
which, belonging to a different order, has a certain priority
over the text and to that extent governs it—in short, a
prearticulation. Within the metaphoric system this prearticulation is expressed as the division of land from sea, the
"unalterable limits" in which the island of truth is "enclosed
by nature itself." This division would be one already established before critical reason comes on the scene, a prearticulation that a critique of reason could, then, only take over and
make directive for itself. Critical reason would travel across
the land, surveying, measuring, putting in order the island
of truth before venturing beyond its shore onto the ocean of
illusion. And though indeed it must be determined before
the tribunal of pure reason that truth is on land and illusion
at sea, the shoreline would be something already established
by nature itself, a prearticulation.

And yet, the determinations reached in the court of pure
reason do not leave this natural prearticulation simply intact.
On the contrary, these determinations in effect withdraw
from that prearticulation such naturalness as would entitle it
to remain something absolutely prior to critical reason—that
is, they withdraw the very concept of an absolute nature.
Surveying the land of truth, the land of the understanding,

and determining the proper place of everything in this land, even of nature itself, critique establishes, as one of its results, that the understanding "is itself the law-giver for nature" (A 125). The prearticulation dividing land from sea, the prearticulation that would be established by nature itself between the domain of understanding and that of dialectical reason, proves in the end to have been itself governed by understanding. Strictly speaking, there is no nature itself, least of all at the very center of reason itself. The prearticulation to which the critical text would be securely hinged and fixed has thus itself begun to turn on that very hinge.

This turning broaches a decisive transformation. Once the prearticulation governing reason's critical and systematic undertaking has proven to have been governed, in turn, by reason itself, once it has proven not to be a gift of nature, it has in effect been transformed into an articulation installed within reason by reason itself. It is a matter of self-articulation, of a certain precritical, presystematic articulation of the field of systematic critique, of a certain opening of reason to itself.

This outcome is related to a certain problem that haunts the very project of a critique of reason and that it must suffice here merely to outline. It is the problem of reason's route to itself, a problem also that threatens to produce an utter rout of reason. It is expressed in a certain torsion intrinsic to that project, a torsion by which the entire project is thrown off center, or, more precisely, a torsion by which the center of the project is displaced outside the text in which that project would be actualized. The torsion expresses an opposition, not to say a rift, that is already operative in the very intention of critical reason. On the one hand, the project of a critique of reason is, in the words of that text, "a call to reason to undertake anew the most difficult of all its tasks, namely, that of self-knowledge" (A xi)—that is, it is a matter of reason's interrogating itself. Such interrogation requires that reason be present to itself, that from the outset an opening of reason to itself be in play. On the other hand, it is precisely a lack of presence to self, a failure in reason's opening to itself, that constitutes the critical problem, that sets reason in conflict with itself and makes of the history of metaphysics a battlefield of endless controversies. If it can be said that the *Critique of Pure Reason,* in actually resolving this conflict, carries out *in its very deed* a certain opening of reason to itself, nevertheless it does not, *in what it says,* vindicate such opening; quite to the contrary, its results, specifically the severe restrictions placed by it on self-knowledge, tend to withdraw the possibility of such opening as is required by critique itself. The results of critique effectively block the route that reason would take back toward the common root, back toward the point at which alterity would be suppressed and reason given absolutely to itself. In short, the *Critique of Pure Reason* moves toward retraction of the very condition of its possibility, toward self-retraction. But Kant does not thematize this peculiar closure; that is, the opening that speaks in the Kantian text and gives that text its explicit articulation, its architectonic—this opening simply remains outside that text, and its exclusion is enforced by the developments in the text. The critical text is secured from the torsion, stabilized, only at the cost of having its voice torn away from it, displaced outside.

And yet, the prearticulation, because of its two-sided character, does not lie simply outside the Kantian text. Indeed, on one side, it coincides with the opening of reason and in this respect lies simply outside the text, aloof, unengaged by the text. But this opening is a self-articulating in and through which certain articulations are instituted, the opening traced in a certain linguistic-conceptual medium. And though this configuration of traces, this exterior side of the prearticulation, also lies outside the text itself, it is nonetheless turned toward that text. In contrast to the remote voice speaking in the text from outside, these traces form the margin of the text, the system of articulations that, posed outside the critical project and its text, frame that text and grant to that project both its problematic and its means of developing that problematic. These marginal traces involve a double reference, one a reference to origin, the other a reference to the text that they frame. Their reference to the opening of reason as their origin is of course what gives them a legitimacy for a critique of reason. But the aloofness of that origin, enforced by critique itself, severely limits the possibility of reenacting the origination so as to fulfill the reference; and, instead of this absolute origin, the origins that actually shine through these traces are historical, that is, certain traditional systems of concepts, metaphors, etc. The traces also carry a reference to the text—or, rather, they are engaged by its development of the problematic, this development recoiling upon them, throwing the frame out of joint, filling the margins with annotations if not retractions. This is why it is never simply a matter of massive, rigid presuppositions: even the most uncritically imported concepts retain a reserve of interdeterminacy sufficient to allow their redetermination through the recoil of the project upon them.

Such is, then, the textuality of the Kantian text: a complex and rigorously structured spacing of origin, margin, and text.[2]

b | Almost the entire text of the *Critique of Pure Reason* is enclosed between two markings of the division of human knowledge into its two stems, as though this marginal trace both opens up and closes off the field of critique. The first marking is located, with utter appropriateness, at the very end of the Introduction, thus immediately preceding the beginning of the *Critique of Pure Reason* proper. It reads:

By way of introduction or anticipation we need only say that there are two stems of human knowledge, namely, *sensibility* and *understanding,* which perhaps spring from a common, but to us unknown root; through the former, objects are given to us, but through the latter they are thought. [A 15/B 29]

The other marking of this division occurs at that point where the final task undertaken in that text, the outlining of the architectonic of pure reason, is about to commence. In that outline it is a matter of projecting the entire system, which at that point has been prepared by critique, a matter of reviewing the complex of articulations that have been fashioned for the system in and through the preceding critique. The text introduces the closing review by reintroducing the opening prearticulation:

We content ourselves here with the completion of our task, namely, merely to project the architectonic of all knowledge arising from *pure reason,* and begin only from the point at which the common root of our power of knowledge divides and throws out two stems, one of which is *reason.* But I understand here by reason the whole higher power of knowledge and thus oppose the rational to the empirical. [A 835/B 863]

Both these passages mark the same prearticulation, though it is, as they show, an opposition that can be marked differently in different contexts: as opposition between sensibility and understanding, as opposition between intuition and thought, or as opposition between the empirical and the rational.

Although both passages affirm a common root, the second even dispensing with the qualifying "perhaps," neither of them, nor any other in the *Critique of Pure Reason*, actually poses the question, What is the common root? Nor does the Kantian text propose, in any explicit way, an answer to that unsaid question. The question of the common root lies even farther outside the text than does the prearticulation that opens and closes that text and is thus at least marked there. The question of the common root is still more marginal.

And yet, this question, remote from the center of Kant's text, is itself precisely a question of center, of a midpoint between reason and sensibility that would at the same time control, reduce, the opposition, the difference, setting the line, as it were, in rotary motion in such a way as to describe a circle, orienting the reduced field to itself as absolute center, the point into which all would be withdrawn, contracted. As a question of center, the question of the common root is central to reason en route, for the common root would be that point that would orient the entire route of radical reason. Central to reason en route, the very sense of *enrouting,* and yet marginal to the Kantian text—thus is indicated the difference between the reductive spacing of enrouting and the spacing of the critical project. Enrouting is focused, centered, on the common root, whereas the critical project is spread, gathered, into the space opened by the opposition between reason and sensibility, hence is decentered with respect to that singular enrouting centered in the question of center. Critique is off center. The circle of enrouting and that of critique are eccentric.

At the center, in the passage from it, let me mark this eccentricity.

c | The eccentricity can be exhibited, played out, in a peculiar spacing of the Kantian text, or, rather, in a certain dynamic play of spacing between that text and the question of the common root. What the play shows is that critique, off center with respect to the question of the common root, assumes—that is, can sustain—no determinate stance with respect to the question and its possible answer. For critique it is a shifting question, one that shifts between different senses, between different answers, between different ways of governing the text. It is a question that, for critique, is intrinsically unstable, irrevocably marginal, a question unassimilable to the critical project.

Four scenes of the play will suffice.

Scene 1 begins with a certain sense of the question, a sense that can be made to stand out by focusing on a peculiar variation in the second of the passages on the common root as compared with the first: the root is characterized not as *gemeinschaftlich* but as *allgemein,* as *die allgemeine Wurzel*— literally, "the general root." The question is, then, one of genus, of the genus to which both stems belong as coordinate species. Once the question has shifted into this sense, once the shift has been made from the metaphorics of root and stem to the conceptuality of genus and species, an answer is easily had. The genus, the root, is representation (*Vorstellung*) (cf. A 320/B 376). This answer governs one of the most crucial opening moves of the *Critique of Pure Reason*, namely, the posing of a parallelism between the Transcendental Aesthetic, devoted to one species of representation (intuition), and the Transcendental Logic, devoted to the other species (thought).

At least from the outset of the Transcendental Logic this parallelism gets brought into question—for example, by the means that prove to be necessary even to define transcendental logic, for which the single distinction between pure and empirical does not, as in the Transcendental Aesthetic, suffice. The developments that follow in the Transcendental Analytic, instead of repairing the rift, serve to make it irreparable. They recoil upon the parallelism, revoking it, ultimately putting the text in opposition to the generic answer to the question of the common root, tearing the text from its margin—or, rather, setting the margin again in motion. The incipient movement within the text can be traced most directly in that peculiar enlargement that the thematic field of the Transcendental Analytic undergoes. Instead of the analysis of pure thought alone, which the strict parallel with the Transcendental Aesthetic would require, the Transcendental Analytic provides an analysis of pure thought in that relation to intuition by which it is rendered objective. The theme becomes twofold, thought *and* intuition; still, though violating the strict parallel in its function of governing the architectonic, this doubling simply reproduces that parallel within the Transcendental Analytic. But the reproduction is soon dismantled: in place of the twofold there emerges a threefold theme—that is, the field is again enlarged so as finally to encompass not only pure thought and pure intuition but also, somehow between them, pure imagination. This final enlargement forces a fundamental revision in the operative architectonic of the Transcendental Analytic and disrupts beyond hope the simple generic parallelism.

The recoil of this textual movement upon the margin of

the text serves to mark the limit of the generic answer to the question of the common root and to shift that question in a different direction, toward a different sense. However, rather than immediately following up that shift, let me, for the sake of economy, return instead to the opening passage concerning the common root and focus on the limit and the shift as they are marked there. In that passage they are marked by the characterization of the common root as "unknown to us." The genus, representation, is not, in any evident sense, unknown to us—hence the limit of the generic answer. On the other hand, there is *one kind* of representation that is indeed unknown to us—hence the shift of the question in a different direction, toward another sense and another answer—a new scene.

Scene 2. What is, then, that kind of representation that is unknown to us, that is confirmed as such by the Kantian text, that is thus entitled to be, in another sense, the common root? Though variously designated, it is invariably presented as a kind of representation that is self-enclosed and unlimited, in contrast to the exposed and limited knowledge to which man finds himself constrained. It is a knowledge not limited by its object, a knowledge that would bring forth its object in the very act of knowing it, a knowing such as one might suppose the divine to possess. But it is a knowing, a kind of representation, that man neither possesses nor knows, a knowing that he can merely *think*.

Although its initial designation as "original intuition" (cf. B 72) tends to suggest that this kind of representation is more an absolutized form of one stem than a common root of the two stems, that designation, shaped to its context in the Transcendental Aesthetic, proves to be only provisional. The subsequently developed designations of it as "intellectual intuition" (cf. B 72, B 159) and as "an understanding that is itself intuitive" (B 145) clearly indicate that it is a matter not of one stem being absolutized to the exclusion of the other but rather of the absolute unity of the two stems. It is a matter of a knowing in which spontaneity and receptivity are fused, a knowing in which the positing of the object and the

intuition of that object form an absolute unity.[3] Such knowing is the common root because it is the absolute unity of the
stems, their original unity. The metaphorics of root and stem
is thus shifted toward the opposition of original unity to
derivative difference, and in place of the common root as
genus there appears the common root as original unity, the
common root in that sense operative in the sense of the
singular *enrouting* of radical reason.

This answer to the question of the common root governs
the global delimitation of the thematic field of critique. To
begin, as the Kantian text says, "only from the point at
which the common root of our power of knowledge divides
and throws out two stems" is to begin only after limitation
and difference have begun to emerge; it is to begin with *finite*
knowing. And having thus begun, the critical analysis continues to be governed in various, mostly covert ways by the
reference to the original unity, thematizing the finite by
opposition to the infinite, remaining within the opposition.

And yet, in another respect critique breaks out of this
opposition—or, more precisely, from its very beginning, *by*
beginning *this side of* the origin, it has already begun to
deconstruct this opposition, to center itself in its very eccentricity. In its beginning, critique has already begun its break
with the common root as original unity—the break that
comes eventually to fruition in the uncovering of another
unity, a nonoriginal unity, a finite unity whose finitude is
not merely the other side of infinitude but at most only an
ecstatic image of that infinitely self-enclosed intellectual
intuition. The limit of the common root as original unity is
thus marked, was in fact already marked in the passages
concerning the common root: it is a matter of the root of
human knowledge, of *our* power of knowledge, of a knowledge this side of the absolute origin, a matter of transition to
a scene this side of the singular enrouting of radical reason.

Scene 3. The shift, transposed from text to margin, installs
the transcendental imagination as common root.

Even with this shift, however, the instability of the ques-

tion of the common root remains in force, unsettling, shift-
ing this answer no less than the others. Indeed, the answer
already begins to veer off in another direction in that very
shift by which it was installed: a unity that supervenes rather
than preceding the moments it would unite is not a root of
which those moments would be stems—that is, a supervenient unity, transcendental imagination as the common
root, would violate the very metaphorics of root and stem.
Even without venturing that rigorous determination (that
would eventually be required) of the extent and structure of
the supervenience belonging to transcendental imagination,
one can be assured of the limit and consequent shift to which
the identification of the common root as transcendental
imagination is subject. For the limit is again marked in one
of the passages concerning the common root, marked by the
same words that marked the limit of the generic answer: the
common root is "unknown to us." Even if the imagination is
something of which, as the Kantian text says, "we are
scarcely ever conscious" (A 78/B 103), that text itself (with
what it presents of a theory of imagination) shows *by its very
deed* that imagination is not unknown to us. A shift is again
under way, still another scene prepared.

Scene 4. Displaced as a question of the nonoriginal unity of
the two stems, displaced from transcendental imagination,
displaced by the marking of the common root as "unknown
to us," the question could again be momentarily secured as a
question of the *unknown* nonoriginal unity of the two stems.
Correspondingly, the common root would then be identified
as transcendental apperception, as the self-positing I, of
which there is, according to the Kantian text, only thought,
not knowledge. German Idealism would now enter the play,
and one appropriate sequel would be to play out the displacement that reason undergoes in the direction of imagination
in the theoretical *Wissenschaftslehre*, the drama of the dove.
On the other hand, it would also suffice to observe that the
shift to transcendental apperception has the effect of transforming one of the stems into the root, thus assimilating one

stem to the other, violating the metaphorics of root and stem, setting the question of the common root again in motion, releasing it from the Kantian text.

The final scene has enacted most transparently the rout(e) of reason, the drama in which reason, one of two stems, becomes the common root only at the cost of having its own sense eroded; the slippage is obtrusive in this scene, reason becoming the mere empty "I think." Displacing itself toward the common root, reason displaces also its very sense, reduces the very space in which it would be delimited. The rout(e) of reason is a compound decentering, and it is in this sense that I shall refer to the *eccentricity of reason*, of reason en route to the common root, of reason in its singular en-routing.

This eccentricity of reason is precisely the undoing of the project of traditional metaphysics as assembled and exposed—in a word, routed—in the Transcendental Dialectic; despite the eccentricity, rational metaphysics would lay claim to utter centeredness, and the entire drama of transcendental dialectic can be read as exhibiting the specific forms of this conflict.

What is most remarkable, on the other hand, is the accord of the critical project with this eccentricity. The very eccentricity of the critical project, its decenteredness into the space of the opposition between reason and sensibility, serves to conform that project to the eccentricity of reason, to make the critique of reason an accordant project. The accord corresponds to a recentering of the critical project in the field of the rout of reason and a reconstituting of that field. The compound decentering, the eccentricity, previously taken to destructure reason would now be reconstituted as the very structuring, the very spacing, of reason. Such transformation of eccentricity into the very spacing of reason is most notable in the temporalizing of reason, that is, in the schematizing of pure understanding.

Accordingly, imagination would not be the common root in the sense of a point toward which reason, one of two stems, would be displaced, a new center, as it were, that would somehow resume the role of reason. Rather, the recentering would, almost paradoxically, serve to deconstruct both centeredness as such and the metaphorics of root and stem. If one were to insist on referring, nevertheless—or, rather, under erasure—to imagination as the (supervenient) common root, one would need not only to distinguish rigorously such rooting from the singular enrouting of reason, that is, to pluralize *enrouting*, but also to abolish with equal rigor the distinction between imagination and that spacing that one might otherwise take to be produced by imagination. Then one would, in the most rigorous way, have begun "only from the point at which the common root of our power of knowledge divides and throws out two stems, one of which is *reason*." One would have begun by letting that point be so effaced as to leave only the merest trace in the spacing of critique.

4 | TREMORINGS—

Withdrawals of the Sublime

> If one is to call sublime . . . the look [*Anblick*] of the
> ocean . . . , one must be able to find the ocean sublime
> merely, as poets do, by what strikes the eye [*nach dem, was
> der Augenschein zeigt*]—if it is regarded at rest, as a clear
> mirror [*Wasserspiegel*] bounded only by the heaven; if it is
> restless, as an abyss [*Abgrund*] threatening to swallow up
> everything.
>
> [I. Kant, *Critique of Judgment*]

First of all, there is a story to be told, or rather, retold, since
Kant himself told it in his text of 1764, *Observations on the
Feeling of the Beautiful and Sublime*. He too was retelling
something he had read, retelling it as an example of the noble
dread—a blend, it seems, of two kinds of sublimity, the
terrifying (*schreckhaft*) and the noble—that a description of
total solitude can instill. It is the story of "Carazan's Dream,"
narrated by the wealthy miser in the first person:

"One evening, as by my lamp I drew up my accounts and
calculated my profits, sleep overpowered me. In this state I saw
the Angel of Death come over me like a whirlwind. He struck
me before I could plead to be spared his terrible stroke. I was
petrified, as I perceived that my destiny throughout eternity
was cast, and that to all the good I had done nothing could be
added, and from all the evil I had committed, not a thing
could be taken away. I was led before the throne of him who
dwells in the third heaven. The glory that flamed before me
spoke to me thus: 'Carazan, your service of God is rejected.
You have closed your heart to the love of man, and have
clutched your treasures with an iron grip. You have lived only
for yourself, and therefore you shall also live the future in

82

eternity alone and removed from all communion with the whole of creation.' At this instant I was swept away by an unseen power and driven through the shining edifice of creation. I soon left countless worlds behind me. As I neared the outermost end of nature, I saw the shadows of the boundless void sink down into the deep before me. A fearful kingdom of eternal silence, loneliness, and darkness! Unutterable horror overtook me at this sight. I gradually lost sight of the last star, and finally the last glimmering ray of light was extinguished in outer darkness! The mortal terrors of despair increased with every moment, just as every moment increased my distance from the last inhabited world. I reflected with unbearable anguish that if ten thousand times a thousand years more should have carried me along beyond the limits of the entire universe I would still always be looking ahead into the immeasurable abyss [*Abgrund*] of darkness, without help or hope of any return."[1]

The range, the sweep, of the story could not be greater: from the throne of glory, on through the shining edifice of creation, on toward the limits of nature, on, endlessly, toward the immeasurable abyss of darkness. Or, rather, one might say, the full course of the story proceeds from an abuse of reason, its reduction to drawing up accounts and calculating profits, its closure to those to whom, as ends in themselves, it ought, as practical, as the very source of the ought, to open. The abuser—the story would perhaps warrant speaking not only of abuse but also, as one might today, of death—is brought to judgment before the tribunal, condemned, one suspects, by reason itself, and then swept away by an unseen power. He is sentenced to solitude, removed not only from all communion in which he might be gathered with others, but set apart, separated, driven out beyond the limit, driven on to such an extent that even the last glimmering ray of light is extinguished, driven on into the immeasurable abyss.

I would like to deal, within a theoretical discourse, with two versions of this story of reason. One version is the Kantian. Here what is decisive is that reason, however much abused, however much drawn into crisis and in need therefore of critique, nevertheless remains essentially intact. The other version of the story is of the sort that one might be more inclined to tell today. It is the story of what happens with the demise of the concept of reason (hence, too, the very concept of concept), or—as one may want to say—of *a* concept of reason, namely, the one that has governed Western metaphysics throughout its course and that is delimited perhaps most rigorously in the first two of Kant's Critiques. What happens when the demand for final unity and self-presence—the demand that it is the very nature of reason both to issue and to fulfill—is not only contested, as in critique, but displaced, set into that very drift that it otherwise would limit? What happens when reason comes to be perpetually interrupted, when a certain separation, a certain spacing, proves incessantly to intervene, dividing what would be unity, even the unity of self-presence, producing and continually reproducing difference?

The story, transposed into theoretical discourse, is one told in the *Critique of Judgment*, specifically in that section that Kant calls "Analytic of the Sublime." It is, then, a story that has to do also, perhaps even primarily, with man's relation to nature, not with his scientifically cognitive relation to nature, not simply with his active, practical relation to nature, but with a certain kind of aesthetic relation to nature, as it has come to be called since Kant. In retelling the Kantian version of the story—in order to broach finally the other version—it will be important to observe just how reason figures into such experience of nature and just how it draws along with it the configuration definitive of metaphysics as such, that which joins the supersensible to the sensible. It is Kant who has perhaps most rigorously traced this figure. It will be important also to see how another figure, one almost effaced, is yet discernible, a figure ever so slightly off-center, prefiguring the other version, the eccentric version, of the story of the sublime.

There are, then, other spacings too in the Kantian text— other spacings in which, as in the schematizing of pure

understanding, the eccentricity of the critical project con-
forms to the eccentricity of reason; other spacings in which
reason mixes with sense without simply violating the opposition; other dimensions of schematism; other workings of
imagination. Indeed such spacings could be regarded as
constituting the sole theme of Kant's "Critique of Aesthetic
Judgment." Hence the strategic position of this text—a
mediating position of course, as Kant himself insists, the
keystone crowning the critical arch; and yet also—at least in
the specific connection that I shall examine—a position ever
so close to the dissolution of every position; a position that
broaches—almost—a rout(e) of reason extending toward an
abyss and transgressing all limits. Everything depends on
whether or not a certain recentering supervenes, on whether
or not a certain guardrail suffices to limit the slippage into
eccentricity. Such recentering, such limiting, is what would
make it possible to bring the critical project to an end. It is
what would make possible such an ending as is marked by
Kant himself at the end of the Preface to the *Critique of
Judgment*, when he writes in first person: "Herewith I end
therefore my whole critical undertaking."[2] It is what would
make possible a definitive ending rather than one extending
indefinitely into an abyss threatening to swallow up everything.

Kant's discourse on the sublime occurs in the interval
between two discourses on the beautiful, the interval in
which imagination is no longer limited to the domain of
understanding and not yet dedicated to the beautiful that
would symbolize morality. One might, then, suppose this
interval to form the site at which the supervention of a
recentering upon the eccentricity of reason would be perhaps
most exposed, most vulnerable, least decisive in quelling the
rout of reason. This is the supposition that I propose to follow
up, though without presuming to close off the possibility of
comparable openings in connection with the discourses on
the beautiful.

It will be a matter, then, of retracing Kant's analysis of the
sublime, adhering as rigorously as possible to his text and yet

marking within that analysis a certain movement that runs throughout the analysis without ever fully governing that analysis, a movement that, if made to govern that analysis, could then—with the slightest twist—turn it into a discourse on the sublime as the site of transgression.

The movement in question is a multiple withdrawal, a withdrawal of the sublime from every site where otherwise it would be delimitable and its spacing brought under control. The engagement of the sublime in the movement can be expressed in the proposition: *Nothing is sublime*. Or, perhaps better, in the proposition: *The sublime would be abysmal*. It will be necessary to specify these propositions at four different levels of Kant's analysis, to show at each level exactly what kind of movement of withdrawal is in play.

a   Nothing is sublime—that is, first of all, no object *simply is* sublime, just as no object *simply is* beautiful. Neither beauty nor sublimity is simply attached to the object, present with it as a positive quality inherent in it. Both are, rather, withdrawn from simple presence in the object, drawn, as it were, back into the space between subject and object.

Later it will appear just how abysmal that space can become. But first it is necessary to reconstitute the Kantian analysis in its full rigor and scope so as to discern in and through that analysis itself the movement of withdrawal from the object.

It is a matter of withdrawal from simple objectivity, from being present as a determination of the phenomenal object, which the *Critique of Pure Reason* establishes as the only legitimate object of theoretical knowledge. Thus, it is a matter of withdrawal from the object of knowledge, a matter of differentiation between aesthetic judgment, in which something would be pronounced beautiful or sublime, and empirical judgment, in which something would be known as possessing some specific determination. Hence, the withdrawal is expressed in the separation between knowledge and aesthetic judgment that Kant sets up at the very outset of the *Critique of Judgment*, where, in reference to "those judgments that concern the beautiful and the sublime of nature or of art," he declares:

For although by themselves alone they contribute nothing at all to the knowledge of things, yet they belong to the faculty of knowledge alone and point to an immediate reference of this faculty to the feeling of pleasure or pain according to some principle a priori. [V]

Note at this stage only one point in this passage: the separation of aesthetic judgment from knowledge is not absolute. On the contrary, the relation is ambivalent, aesthetic judgment belonging to the faculty of knowledge, that is, judgment as such constituting one of the faculties of knowledge, along with understanding and reason; and yet not contributing to the knowledge of things, as Kant repeats emphatically near the end of the Introduction: "Aesthetic judgment contributes nothing toward the knowledge of its objects" (E VIII). Because the separation is not absolute, it is a matter of withdrawal rather than a definitive change of the domain of determination. It will be important to observe how this separation is developed and reaffirmed in the course of Kant's analyses, especially as another faculty comes to be integrated into the analysis, namely imagination, which, quite remarkably, is missing from Kant's introductory classification of the faculties.

The withdrawal is expressed positively in the reference of both the beautiful and the sublime to aesthetic judgment. Let me focus for the moment on the beautiful, since in this connection its constitution does not differ from that of the sublime and since, more generally, its analysis needs to be outlined in order later to be able to introduce the analysis of the sublime by a series of differentiations from the beautiful. What, then, is beautiful? Nothing is beautiful, nothing in and of itself—in Kant's words: "Beauty is not a characteristic of the object considered for itself" (§ 58). Just as its very determination as an object involves reference to the subject, so likewise—Kant himself draws the parallel (cf. § 58)—the determination of an object as beautiful involves—though at a different level, one that it is necessary to keep distinct from that of objectivity as such—reference back to the subject; and thus from the very outset the Kantian analysis of the beautiful belongs quite coherently to the most generally defining gesture of Kantian thought, the turn toward the subject as ground, Kant's so-called Copernican revolution. An object is, then, determined as beautiful not in and of itself but rather in reference to the subject: "Yet beauty, without reference to the feeling of the subject, is nothing for itself [*für sich nichts ist*]" (§ 9). The analysis of the beautiful must therefore follow up this reference back to the subject, regarding the beautiful as the correlate of a certain judgmental activity of the subject, which also, Kant has indicated, is linked somehow to feeling. An analysis of the beautiful must be primarily an analysis of such judgment, which Kant calls judgment of taste (*Geschmacksurteil*): "What is required in order to call an object beautiful must be discovered by an analysis of judgments of taste" (§ 1n.). It is with the judgment of taste or, more generally, with aesthetic judgment that one must begin.

What, then, is to be understood by judgment and what kind of judgment is an aesthetic judgment? Kant's introductory definition appears straightforward: "Judgment in general is the faculty of thinking the particular as contained under the universal" (E IV). A division into two major types follows immediately: if the universal is given along with the particular so that judgment consists then in subsuming the latter under the former, the judgment is determinant (*bestimmend*); but if only the particular is given so that judgment requires also that the universal under which the particular is to be subsumed be found, the judgment is reflective (*reflektierend*). In the latter type there is a connection with purposiveness in a very general sense: The referral of the particular to the previously nongiven universal is a representing of that particular as purposive, as conforming to an order of universality, as exhibiting such order as would be required were it to be legislated by an understanding (cf. E V).

The beautiful is determined as the correlate of a certain type of reflective judgment, namely, a judgment of taste. This type of reflective judgment needs therefore to be differentiated; this requires specifying the exact character assumed by the subsumption of the particular under the universal that is to be discovered for it, that is, specifying the character of the movement in which judgment, proceeding from the given particular, ascends in search of a universal under which to subsume the particular. Two differentiations, that is, specifications, are required. First, the movement from particular to universal may proceed either in an objective direction, in which case the universal has the character of an objective concept or purpose and the judgment is a teleological judgment, or in a subjective direction, in which case something universal in the subject must come into play as the term of the ascent. But what is there that is universal in the subject? What is subjective universality? It is nothing less than the very faculties of universality, that engagement by which universality, conceptuality, is operative in experience. Subjective universality, the operation of universality in the subject, is simply the engagement of understanding and imagination, their operation as it works to bring the manifold of intuition under the categories. This operation is something not marked by the particularity of the subject, is something common to all, a *sensus communis* (cf. §§ 20–21). A reflective judgment in which the particular is referred to such subjective universality is an aesthetic judgment.

The final differentiation is between the two types of aesthetic judgment as the correlates of which the beautiful and the sublime, respectively, are determined. Let me continue to focus on the beautiful, postponing the more exacting interrogation of the sublime that will eventually be necessary. The judgment of taste, to which the beautiful is correlative, involves three constituent phases, three structural moments. Two of the moments derive immediately from the general structure of the reflective judgment: a particular must be given, that is, *apprehended*; and there must be a movement by which the apprehended particular is referred to the subject's cognitive faculties, that is, what I shall call a *reflection*. The third movement is that *feeling* of pleasure that is produced through such judgment.

It is through the specific character of each of the three moments that the specific character of the judgment of taste is most readily approached. The character of the first moment, that of apprehension, is outlined most succinctly by a phrase that I shall excerpt from a complex passage in the "Introduction," a passage whose complexity will have to be unfolded gradually. The phrase is: "Apprehension of forms in the imagination [*Auffassung der Formen in die Einbildungskraft*]" (E VII). Three features of the apprehension operative in the judgment of taste are marked in this phrase. First, the particular object, the thing that would be determined as beautiful through the judgment, is *merely apprehended*; beyond that mere apprehension there is no further involvement with the object—that is, there is a certain detachment from it, a disinterest. Most notably, the apprehension occurs "without reference to a concept"—that is, it involves no subsumption of what is apprehended under a concept, hence no knowledge. The phrase indicates, second, what it is that is apprehended and, in being apprehended, is detached, as it were, from the object: what is apprehended is the *mere form* of the object, "not the matter of its representation, as sensation." Finally, the apprehension is said to occur "in the imagination"; *imagination* is the agent of the apprehension, the faculty operative in it.

Another of the structural moments of the judgment of taste is the feeling of pleasure that is bound up with the judgment proper. Let me cite now the first part of that passage from which the above excerpt was taken:

If pleasure is bound up with the mere apprehension (*apprehensio*) of the form of an object of intuition, without reference of it to a concept for a definite cognition, then the representation is thereby not referred to the object, but simply to the subject, and the pleasure can express nothing else than its harmony [*Angemessenheit*] with the faculties of knowledge that are in play in the reflective judgment, and so far as they are in play, and hence can only express a subjective formal purposiveness of the object. [E VII]

In the judgment of taste the apprehended form is—as in all aesthetic judgment—referred to the subject. The pleasure bound up with the apprehension, with the judgment, simply expresses a harmony exhibited between the apprehended form and those faculties of knowledge to which it is referred; the pleasure expresses, in other words, a purposiveness of the object with respect to the subject, its conformity to subjective universality.

There is still another structural moment, indeed the central moment, the reflection itself, the referral of the apprehended form to the cognitive faculties in such a way that a certain harmony can be exhibited. In order to begin circumscribing the character of the harmony that gets exhibited, let me cite the immediate continuation of the passage quoted above:

For that apprehension of forms in the imagination can never take place without the reflective judgment, though undesignedly [or unintentionally (*unabsichtlich*)], at least comparing them[3] with its faculty of referring intuitions to concepts. If, now, in this comparison the imagination (as the faculty of a priori intuitions) is placed [*versetzt*] by means of a given representation undesignedly [*unabsichtlich*] in agreement with the understanding, as the faculty of concepts, and thereby a feeling of pleasure is aroused, the object must then be regarded as purposive for the reflective judgment. [E VII]

Here a structural order is established, one by which the reflective moment is set at the center of the structure of the judgment of taste, taking up what is provided by apprehension so as then to produce a feeling of pleasure.

Reflection involves a certain comparison (*Vergleichung*), a comparing of the apprehension of forms in the imagination *with* the faculty of referring intuitions to concepts. Now, this faculty is just the understanding in its empirical function. Hence, reflection is charged with comparing, undesignedly, the way in which forms are apprehended in imagination *with* the way in which they would be taken up by understanding, though—and this is of utmost significance—they are not actually taken up into the definitive workings of empirical understanding, not taken up and conceptualized; no definite concept (hence no knowledge) is generated in aesthetic judgment. On the basis of the passage cited, one could, then, regard the agreement (*Einstimmung*) that can come to be exhibited through the reflection as a harmony between the operations of imagination and of understanding. If in a given case such agreement is exhibited, then a feeling of pleasure is aroused; and the object in relation to whose apprehension the harmony has been exhibited may be regarded as purposive with respect to the subject's faculties, that is, as beautiful.

The character of the judgment of taste may, then, be outlined as follows: in the case of a beautiful object, the apprehended form is referred to the cognitive faculties in such a way that a harmony is displayed and a feeling of pleasure produced.

There is need to press somewhat further with respect to at least two points in this outline: first, regarding the reflection proper and, second, regarding the harmony or agreement. More specifically, the reflection needs to be clarified especially with regard to its agency. What faculty is it that performs the reflection? Is it understanding or imagination or simply a faculty of judgment that would be distinct from understanding and imagination? And then, what precisely is the character of the harmony that can come to be exhibited through the reflection? And what is the character of the exhibiting? To what faculty, to what state of mind, is the agreement disclosed?

The harmony that can come to be exhibited is preeminently one between the operations of imagination and of understanding. On the other hand, there are several passages in which Kant stresses rather the harmony between the object and the cognitive faculties of the subject. For example, in the same context as the passage cited above, he writes of the "harmony [*Zusammenstimmung*] of the object with the faculties of the subject" (E VII); or, more specifically, of "the purposive harmony [*zweckmäßige Übereinstimmung*] of an object (whether a product of nature or of art) with the relation between the cognitive faculties (the imagination and the understanding), a harmony that is requisite for every empirical cognition" (E VII). The point is, first of all, that an object whose apprehension leads, through reflection, to the display of a harmony between the operations of imagination and of understanding proves thereby to be purposive with respect to the subject's faculties, proves to have a purposive relation to those faculties in their interplay. But it needs also to be noted that this very relation is itself identified as a harmony. More closely considered, this is not so much another moment of harmony, another sense that would need to be distinguished from the preeminent sense, but rather it only serves to indicate the complexity of the latter. In this regard, one need only consider that the object enters, as it were, into the judgment only as form, through the apprehension of its form in imagination, that is, in and through the operation of imagination. Hence, the relation between the object and the faculties is not a simple external relation of the object to the subject but rather is a relation in which one faculty, namely, imagination, is already involved. Thus, to say that the object is in harmony with the faculties is already to refer to the harmony between those faculties, that is, to the preeminent sense of harmony.

Let me turn now to another passage in order to clarify more definitively the character of the display of harmony and of the reflection that can issue in such display:

The cognitive powers, which are set in play [*ins Spiel gesetzt werden*] by this representation, are here in free play [*in einem freien Spiel*], because no definite concept limits them to a definite rule of cognition.[§ 9]

In connection with this passage several points need to be considered.

The first point concerns the character of the harmony that can come to be displayed between imagination and understanding. The passage indicates that such harmony is not some static condition but a *free play*. The point is that the apprehended form is not simply brought under a concept (as would be the case in empirical judgment), but rather, in the terms that Kant uses in this context, the given representation is referred to cognition in general. Hence, it is not a matter of the imaginally apprehended form being brought under a concept of understanding in such a way that in the end the understanding would, as it were, rule over imagination; rather, their relation is one of free play, that is, they "are mutually conducive [*einander wechselseitig beförderlich sind*]."[4] It is as though the form apprehended in imagination were reflected to understanding, only to be cast back upon imagination, from which it would be reflected anew, the unlimited reiteration setting the two faculties in resonance.

The passage mentions, second, that "the cognitive powers . . . are set in play by this representation." What representation? The representation characterized in the immediately preceding sentence as "a given representation," as the representation that is referred to cognition in general. What sets the faculties in play is just the form apprehended in imagination. Other passages are more explicit—for example, one from the same context in which Kant writes of "the animation [*Belebung*] of both faculties (imagination and understanding) to *indeterminate* but yet, through the inducement [*Anlaß*] of the given representation, harmonious [*einhellig*] activity." The point is that the reflection from which the harmonious interplay can issue is not performed by some agency that would supervene upon the process; rather, it is already under way with the very apprehension, provoked, induced, by the apprehension of form in imagination. One

could say, orienting the result to the operation of imagination: in the apprehension imagination is in play and already,
from the outset, in interplay with understanding.

But still, supposing there proves to be a harmonious free
play, how is it experienced? To what faculty is that harmonious play displayed? To what state of mind is it exhibited,
disclosed? This question is addressed by the immediate continuation of the passage being primarily considered:

Hence the state of mind [*Gemütszustand*] in this representation
must be a feeling [*Gefühl*] of the free play of the representational powers in a given representation with reference to a cognition in general.

The point is, then, that the harmony, the harmonious free
play, is *felt*. The point is even more directly expressed in
another context in which Kant explains that the determining ground of aesthetic judgment is "the feeling (of internal sense) of that harmony in the play of the mental powers"
(§ 15). It is, then, to feeling—feeling of the harmony and
freedom of the free play⁵—that the harmonious free play is
disclosed as such.

A final point: this feeling is to be identified with that
feeling of pleasure that is produced in aesthetic judgment.
Kant writes:

The consciousness of the mere formal purposiveness in the play
of the subject's cognitive powers, in a representation through
which an object is given, is the pleasure itself. . . . [§ 12]

Or again, he writes of "sensing [*empfinden*] with pleasure the
representational state [*Vorstellungszustand*]" (§ 39)—that is,
feeling with pleasure the harmony and freedom of the free
play set in motion by the apprehension of form in imagination. Here especially an indication is given of just how
complex the structure of this feeling is: in one dimension a
double intentionality with respect to the harmonious free
play; but also, in another, nonintentional dimension, a feeling *of pleasure*. But the point that is essential to the analysis of

the judgment of taste is simply that there is not first an experience of the harmonious free play and then, as a consequence, as a product, a feeling of pleasure; rather the feeling of harmonious free play *is* the feeling of pleasure. The feeling of pleasure is thus not some extrinsic product of the judgment of taste but an integral moment in its structure.

Such is in outline Kant's first discourse on the beautiful, the one that precedes his discourse on the sublime. Or rather, what I have outlined is the analysis of the structure of the judgment of taste, extracting that analysis from a much richer discourse, passing over, perhaps most notably, the way in which certain developments toward the end of that discourse—such as the introduction of the distinction between free and dependent beauty—prepare the way for the second Kantian discourse on the beautiful, the one that follows the discourse on the sublime, the one that is addressed to the questions of genius and of aesthetic ideas. But it is to the discourse on the sublime that this outline is to open, specifically, to that level of the movement of withdrawal that is common to the beautiful and the sublime.

In the analysis that I have outlined there is one peculiar development, a kind of shift or displacement, that needs to be marked. The development is related to the separation between aesthetic judgment and knowledge that is set up by Kant at the very outset of the *Critique of Judgment*, the separation that expresses the withdrawal of the beautiful and the sublime from simple presence in the object, their withdrawal from simple objectivity. It has already been observed that this separation is not absolute; indeed a certain connection between the aesthetic (in its specific sense) and the cognitive is posited in the very conjunction "aesthetic judgment," in the very conception of the beautiful and the sublime as correlative to a kind of judgment, to a certain operation of a cognitive faculty. Furthermore, the connection is strengthened by the strongly cognitive sense in which Kant takes judgment at the outset: judgment as the subsumption of a particular under a universal.

The development that I would like to mark involves a certain erosion of the structure of reflective judgment in its initial, cognitively related sense. For though aesthetic judgment too would consist in the subsumption of a given particular under a universal that has to be sought out for it, it turns out, almost at the beginning of the analysis, that the universal to which the particular (the apprehended form) is to be referred is not at all a universal in the usual, cognitive sense of a universal *concept*. On the contrary, it proves to be quite essential to aesthetic judgment (specifically, to judgment of taste, though later it will appear that the results extend to judgment of the sublime, hence to aesthetic judgment in general)—it proves to be essential that there not be any subsumption of the particular under a universal concept. The particular is referred not to a universal concept but to the faculties of universality; and though these faculties can indeed be termed cognitive faculties, that interplay of them into which the particular is taken up is not a matter of knowledge but rather is only analogous to their way of operating in cognition.

A similar erosion of the judgmental structure can be discerned in the reflection, the central moment in which the particular is referred to the universal. What the analysis shows is that the reflection is not carried out by some agency that would supervene upon the process, connecting the imaginally apprehended particular form, on the one hand, with the operation of universality, the play of imagination and understanding, on the other. It is not a matter of an additional faculty that one would want to call judgment proper and to distinguish from imagination, understanding, and reason. In this sense there is no separate faculty of judgment operative in the judgment of taste.[6] Instead of being carried out by such a supervenient faculty, the referral of the apprehended form to the play of imagination and understanding is already released by the apprehension itself.

One could stress even more the role that imagination comes to assume as the analysis proceeds. What determines this role is the dual operation that imagination turns out to have in the judgment of taste, its apprehensive operation and its operation in the free play with understanding. Granted this dual operation, one could say that the space between apprehension and the free play—the spacing of the judgment of taste—comes in the course of the analysis to be assimilated to imagination; it comes to be determined as two moments within the operation of imagination. One could then regard the judgment in the judgment of taste as assimilated to imagination, displaced by imagination, transformed into an operation of imagination.

In any case, the judgment in the judgment of taste undergoes a certain erosion, an effacement that could be displayed by a writing under erasure: ~~judgment~~ of taste. The result of such erosion is to strengthen the separation between the aesthetic (I shall continue to use this in the specific sense related to the beautiful and the sublime) and the cognitive. What initially appeared to be an essentially cognitive moment at the center of aesthetic judgment has proven in the course of the analysis to be quite distinct from the operation of cognition, at most analogous to it. If, in view of this effacement, one still insisted on retaining a certain cognitively structured aesthetic judgment—in the form of the singular judgment, "This object is beautiful"—such a judgment could only be regarded as a detached image of an aesthetic judgment in the more genuine sense, that is, as a duplication or expression of what would already have been disclosed in and through what could be called the aesthetic operation proper.

The erosion of the judgment in the judgment of taste serves to further the separation between the aesthetic and the cognitive and hence to underscore the withdrawal of the beautiful from simple objectivity. In the judgment of taste it is not a matter of a beautiful object that would simply be present as such and that would then in the aesthetic judgment be represented as beautiful. Rather it is a matter of an operation that could be said to constitute the object as beautiful, provided such constitution is not taken as creation of the form by virtue of which the object comes to be determined as beautiful; rather, such constitution is to be regarded as a matter of first letting the object present itself as beautiful. Such an operation is essentially different from cognition, especially insofar as knowledge involves submission to an already present object.[7] One way of marking that difference—though at the risk of transgressing too quickly the limits of the Kantian problematic—would be to regard the aesthetic operation as the very opening of the space in which the beautiful can shine forth—that is, as the spacing of τὸ ἐκφανέστατον.

b | But nothing is sublime—that is, no object can be sublime even in the limited sense in which an object can be beautiful. Whereas judgment of taste, though not submitted to a beauty simply present in the object, still determines the object as beautiful, judgment in the case of the sublime does not determine any object as sublime—at least not in the proper sense of that word—but only makes use of the object for a disclosure essentially independent of nature. Kant draws the contrast quite explicitly:

> We must seek a ground outside ourselves for the beautiful of nature, but seek it for the sublime merely in ourselves and in our way of thought, which introduces [*hineinbringt*] sublimity into the representation of nature. [§ 23]

The sublime is more withdrawn from the object than is the beautiful, withdrawn more decisively into the subject.

At the most general level the structure of judgment of the sublime corresponds to that of judgment of taste. It is a reflective judgment, one detached from mere sensation and from definite concepts. It is an aesthetic judgment centered in the reference from imaginal apprehension to a faculty of concepts. It is singular, and yet, through the reference to the operation of universality in the subject, it is "universally valid for every subject" (§ 23). As such, it too is dissociated from knowledge, making "no claim to any knowledge of the object" (§ 23)—that is, the sublime too is withdrawn from the object of knowledge.

And yet, it is more withdrawn. To begin tracing the further withdrawal will require thematizing—as Kant does at some length—the way in which the judgment of the sublime differs from that of the beautiful. Let me focus, then, in turn, on each of the three moments that compose the structure common to all aesthetic judgments, differentiating each moment of the judgment of the sublime from the corresponding moment in the judgment of taste.

It is in the character of what is apprehended that the apprehension belonging to the judgment of the sublime differs from the corresponding moment of the judgment of taste. In the case of the beautiful, imagination apprehends "the form of the object, which consists in delimitation [*Begrenzung*]" (§ 23); in this case, then, the object must be one that is delimited, and what is apprehended is the form that delimits the object. The case of the sublime is different: "The sublime, on the other hand, is to be found also in a formless object" (§ 23); in this case, then, the object can be formless, can lack—yet does not necessarily lack[8]—a form that would delimit it. What is it, then, that is actually apprehended in the case of the sublime? Certainly not that which Kant previously opposed to form, namely, "the matter of its representation, as sensation"; for the judgment of the sublime is no less detached from mere sensation than is the judgment of taste. Hence, what is apprehended must, as in the other case, have to do with form, even in those instances in which the object is formless. What is essential is that the object, whether formed or formless, be such that "in it or by occasion of it unlimitedness [*Unbegrenztheit*] is represented" (§ 23). Thus, what is apprehended is a certain formal unlimitedness, a certain exceeding of form, a certain breaching of whatever delimitedness the object might possess. Such excess would not be restricted to formless objects—even if it were possible for an object to be utterly

formless; and indeed one might well suppose that its representation would always require in the object a certain
breaching, a certain interchange between form and formlessness. In any event, it is quite decisive that even in the initial
moment, that of apprehension, the sublime involves
movement; again and again Kant will draw the contrast between the sublime and the beautiful by means of the opposition between movement and rest. What this suggests is
equally decisive: the character of what is apprehended, its
character as movement, as an exceeding of form, serves to
suggest how futile will be every attempt to circumscribe a
site where the sublime would be delimitable and its spacing
brought under control, especially if that site is sought in the
object and even if, as with the site of the beautiful, allowance
is made for a certain constitution of that site by the judgment.

In what kind of objects, in what region of objects, is such
movement, such unlimitedness, to be apprehended? The
purity of aesthetic judgment, that is, its detachment from
concepts, requires that a certain privilege be given to raw
nature:

One must not exhibit [*aufzeigen*] the sublime in products of art
(e.g., buildings, pillars, etc.), where a human purpose [*Zweck*]
determines the form as well as the size, nor in things of nature
the concepts of which bring with them a definite purpose (e.g., ani-
mals with a known natural destination), but in raw nature [*an
der rohen Natur*]. . . . [§ 26]

Even if there be no question of purpose, no question of a
teleological concept, nature is still to be privileged over art,
its privilege prescribed in any case by a certain order of
mimesis, which—at least in the Analytic of the Sublime—
Kant merely invokes without preparation or development:

. . . here, as is right, we bring into consideration first of all
only the sublime in natural objects (that of art is always limited by the conditions of agreement with nature).
[§ 23]

Those things that one customarily calls sublime, those

things in which, more precisely, the exceeding of form can be apprehended, are the things of raw nature, the things of nature most removed from purpose and formal delimitation. Thus, "nature excites the ideas of the sublime, for the most part, in its chaos or in its wildest and most irregular disorder and desolation, provided that magnitude and power let themselves be seen [*wenn sich nur Größe und Macht blicken läßt*]" (§ 23). It is, then, in a certain vision of the magnitude and power of raw nature that one apprehends that exceeding of form that initiates the judgment of the sublime. In the first case, it is a matter of the mathematically sublime—for example, "shapeless masses of mountains piled in wild disorder upon one another with their pyramids of ice, or the gloomy raging sea" (§ 26). In the other case, the vision of power in the things of raw nature, it is a matter of the dynamically sublime—for example, "bold, overhanging, and, as it were, threatening rocks; clouds piled up in the sky, moving with lightning flashes and thunder peals; volcanoes in all their violence of destruction; hurricanes with their track of devastation; the boundless ocean in a state of tumult; a high waterfall of a mighty river" (§ 28).[9]

In the judgment of the sublime, no less than in the judgment of taste, the moment of reflection is continuous with that of apprehension. Its general character is indicated in the continuation of the passage already cited in connection with the moment of apprehension:

The sublime, on the other hand, is to be found also in a formless object insofar as in it or by occasion of it unlimitedness is represented, and yet its totality is added in thought [*hinzugedacht wird*]. Thus the beautiful appears [*scheint*] to be taken as the presentation [*Darstellung*] of an indefinite concept of understanding, the sublime as that of a like concept of reason. [§ 23]

Reflection proceeds, then, *from* the unlimitedness, the exceeding of form, that is apprehended by imagination *to* a totality posited in thought, the totality of that object whose very unlimitedness has been apprehended. But the faculty that preeminently posits totality is, as the *Critique of Pure Reason* demonstrates, reason. Thus, the reflection at the center of the judgment of the sublime may be regarded as proceeding from imagination, which apprehends, to reason, which posits totality—in contrast to the reflective moment of the judgment of taste, which proceeds from imagination to understanding.

The continuity between apprehension and reflection is to be stressed. It is expressed in the way in which the division of the sublime into mathematical and dynamical, which initially appeared to be merely a matter of two different kinds of apprehension, turns out to be codetermined by the moment of reflection. Specifically, Kant indicates that the reflection can proceed "either to the faculty of cognition or to the faculty of desire" (§ 24)—that is, according to the classificatory scheme of the Introduction to the *Critique of Judgment*, to reason in either of its two capacities, as a faculty of knowledge or as a faculty of desire, in short, as theoretical reason or as practical reason. In the first case, that is, reflection of apprehended magnitude to theoretical reason, it is a matter of the mathematically sublime; in the other case, reflection of apprehended power to practical reason, it is a matter of the dynamically sublime.

The moment of feeling as it occurs in the judgment of the sublime also differs quite decisively from the corresponding moment in the judgment of taste. Instead of a simply pleasant feeling of the harmonious free play, there is emotion (*Rührung*), that is, "the feeling of a momentary checking of the vital powers and a consequent stronger outflow of them" (§ 23). In contrast to the restful contemplation characteristic of the judgment of taste, the judgment of the sublime involves a certain *movement* of the mind (cf. § 24) and a feeling that corresponds with such movement:

As the mind is not merely attracted by the object but is ever being alternately repelled, the satisfaction in the sublime does not so much involve a positive pleasure as admiration or respect [*Bewunderung oder Achtung*], which deserves to be called negative pleasure. [§ 23]

One could say, then, that the judgment of the sublime is throughout a matter of movement or, rather, of the interrelation of movements: the movement apprehended by imagination in its own movement of being alternately attracted by and repelled from the object; the referral of what is apprehended to reason; and the affective movement, the emotion, that to some degree pulsates in accord with the initial movement in which imagination is attracted and repelled, that is, shaken, thrown into a state of tremulous excitement, overcome by a tremor, or—activating it still more by fabricating a corresponding verb—set tremoring. But at this stage of the analysis Kant does not yet introduce the word that I shall undertake to translate by having recourse to this fabrication.

Kant expresses the difference between the judgment of the sublime and the judgment of taste not only through the differentiation of the corresponding moments but also in a more global way, that is, in terms of the purposiveness of the relation exhibited in the judgment between what is apprehended and the faculties of the subject. In the case of the judgment of taste there is straightforward purposiveness: the apprehended form proves to be harmonious with the faculties in play, imagination and understanding. But in the case of the judgment of the sublime matters are more complex and the purposiveness anything but straightforward. On the one hand, the judgment of the sublime is an aesthetic judgment, and its character as such prescribes that the object should prove to be purposive, harmonious, with respect to the faculties of the subject; such purposiveness is what would render the judgment aesthetic and what would exhibit its object as the object of an aesthetic judgment. However, such is not the character of the object that is involved in the judgment of the sublime, the object that one customarily calls sublime:

On the other hand, that which excites in us . . . the feeling of the sublime may appear, as regards its form, to violate purpose with respect to our judgment [*zweckwidrig für unsere Urteils-*

kraft], to be unsuited to our presentative faculty [*Darstellungs-vermögen*], and, as it were, to do violence to the imagination; and yet it is judged to be only the more sublime. [§ 23]

In the case of the sublime, then, the object—an object, in the first place, of raw nature—appears to violate rather than display purposiveness; it appears to do violence to the imagination, to be unsuited to, unharmonious with, the faculties of the subject. Hence, a contradiction emerges: the sublime must be, and yet is not, purposive with respect to the faculties. Kant in effect resolves the contradiction by declaring that the object itself is not sublime in the proper sense, that it is not "the authentically sublime [*das eigentliche Erhabene*]" (§ 23), but that it merely "is fit for the presentation [*Darstellung*] of a sublimity" (§ 23). The sublimity that can thus come to be presented does not lie in the object, nor is the purposiveness that is authentically displayed a purposiveness in nature. The sublime proper, the authentically sublime, is to be found not in the object, not in nature, but—if it is, in the end, to be found at any site—in the subject itself. Nothing in nature is sublime. The sublime is withdrawn into the subject.

C | The question is whether, withdrawn into the subject, the sublime assumes the form of a positive state that could be theoretically delimited, confined to a determinable site, and its spacing brought under control. For developing this question, the analysis of the structure of the judgment of the sublime must press further, especially into the interrelation of the various movements that have been found to compose that structure. For such an incursion a more minute analysis of the three structural—or, more precisely, kinetic—moments is needed.

The previous analysis has indicated not only that apprehension is of two types, depending on whether it is oriented to magnitude or to power, but also that these two types of apprehension link up with two different types of reflection so as to produce the two distinct types of judgments of the sublime, those of the mathematically sublime and of the dynamically sublime. This differentiation and the characters of each of the two specific types of apprehension need to be examined more closely. For it is not merely a matter of apprehending magnitude and power, respectively, as simple, positive determinations of the object customarily (though improperly) called sublime. Rather, what is apprehended is a certain unlimitedness, a certain exceeding, in each of the two orders, that of magnitude and that of power. The object must, then, be one that exceeds others in size or might, its magnitude or its power superior to that of others.

In the case of the mathematically sublime, it is a matter of superiority in magnitude. And yet, there is in this case no exact determination of that magnitude, the apprehension or estimation not positing it as a finally determinate positive quantity. For in the estimation there is operative a standard that, though assumed to be the same for everyone, is "merely subjective"—as, for example, the average size of the men known to us, or that of trees, of houses, of mountains (cf. § 25). Thus, in the case of the mathematically sublime the apprehension is decidedly nonmathematical. Indeed Kant contrasts aesthetic estimation of magnitudes, based on subjective standards, with mathematical (or logical) estimation, which would be based on a definite measure. But then, having drawn the contrast, Kant proceeds to disrupt it by insisting on the essential impossibility of an estimation of magnitude that would be purely and rigorously mathematical, since "we can never have a first or fundamental measure, and therefore can never have a determinate concept of a given magnitude" (§ 26). Since the measure must always finally be aesthetic, not mathematical, Kant concludes that "all estimation of magnitude of objects of nature is in the end aesthetic (that is, subjectively and not objectively determined)" (§ 26).

Whereas for the mathematical estimation of magnitude (within the limits that such is possible) there is no max-

imum, numbers extending to infinity, for aesthetic estimation, on the other hand, there is always a maximum, a
greatest. The necessity of such a maximum is to be understood in reference to the dual operation that Kant ascribes to
imagination as the agency of apprehension of magnitude.
The first operation he terms simply apprehension (*Auffassung, apprehensio*). Such apprehension proper, as it is operative
in the judgment of the mathematically sublime, is necessarily in every instance partial, that is, apprehension proper
proceeds sequentially; for it is oriented to magnitude that
exceeds, that is, the kinetically superior. The other operation
is necessary precisely because of this partial, sequential character of the apprehension. Kant calls it comprehension
(*Zusammenfassung, comprehensio*). Through this operation the
movement of exceeding is, as it were, assumed—that is, it is
the operation of gathering, oriented toward assembling the
parts into a whole, toward presenting the object in its full
magnitude. But it is precisely the characer of the judgment
of the mathematically sublime that its apprehensive moment
(involving the dual operation) does not issue in an apprehension of a determinate whole but rather takes up a
certain exceeding in the order of magnitude. Hence, though
apprehension proper can go on—sequentially—ad infinitum, proceeding from one part to the next, comprehension attains a certain maximum:

> For when apprehension has gone so far that the partial repre-
> sentations of sensible intuition initially apprehended begin to
> vanish in the imagination, while the latter proceeds to the ap-
> prehension of others, then it loses as much on the one side as
> it gains on the other; and in comprehension there is a max-
> imum beyond which it cannot go. [§ 26]

Comprehension—hence, the entire phase of apprehension in
imagination—encounters a limit, a limit to what can be
gathered up toward a whole.

Kant offers two examples. They are curious ones, sights
that Kant himself never saw, one of them identified as an
example of the sublime in order to explain something read in

a travel book, the other similarly put forth in relation to a certain hearsay ("Wie man erzählt"). What is perhaps even more curious is that they are not *pure* examples, not things in raw nature, but rather products of art, indeed exemplary products of art.

On the other hand, they are examples that serve almost perfectly to illustrate the character of the apprehensive moment in the judgment of the mathematically sublime, specifically, to illustrate the way in which something customarily (though improperly) called mathematically sublime exceeds in the order of magnitude the imaginal capacity to comprehend it. The first example is that of the pyramids: if one is stationed close enough to apprehend the parts distinctly, then imagination proves incapable of gathering the whole:

> The eye requires some time to complete the apprehension of the tiers from the bottom up to the apex, and then the first tiers are always partly forgotten before the imagination has taken up the last, and so the comprehension is never complete. [§ 26]

The second example is that of St. Peter's in Rome:

> For there is here a feeling of the inadequacy of his imagination for presenting the ideas of a whole, wherein imagination reaches its maximum, and, in striving to surpass it, sinks back into itself, but thereby is transposed [*versetzt wird*] into an emotional satisfaction. [§ 26]

The second example goes beyond merely illustrating, as does the first, the way in which the relation between apprehension proper and comprehension imposes a limit on the latter. In the example of St. Peter's what is illustrated—or rather, traced—is the course, the trajectory, followed by imagination in its comprehensive striving to gather all the apprehended parts up into the whole. The course involves imagination's reaching its maximal comprehension, striving to exceed it, failing, and thus sinking back into itself, being transposed then into a certain satisfaction. On this course it is a matter of pushing "the comprehension of the many in an intuition to the limit of the faculty of imagination" (§ 26), a matter of a "striving toward comprehension [that] surpasses the power [*Vermögen*] of imagination" (§ 26). It is a course on which imagination thus "exhibits its own limits" (§ 27). Hence, in the striving toward the whole and in the failure to attain that whole comprehensively, there occurs what could be called an *experience of limitation*. It is not only a matter of imagination's reaching its limit, but it is also, in its very way of reaching that limit, an experiencing of the excess of nature, of its exceeding that capacity of the human imagination to grasp, that is, comprehend, it. This excess of nature, disclosed only in the experience of limitation and irreducible to a determinate magnitude—this excess is the unlimitedness, the infinity, of nature:

Nature is therefore sublime in those of its appearances whose intuition brings with it the idea of its infinity. This last can occur in no other way than through the inadequacy of the greatest striving of our imagination to estimate the magnitude of an object. [§ 26]

Hence, the experience of limitation that occurs within the apprehensive moment of the judgment of the mathematically sublime is both an experience of the limitation of imagination and, correlatively, of the excess of nature, of its unlimitedly surpassing the imaginal capacity to grasp it. It is, then, an experience in which is disclosed the *difference* between unlimited—or, more precisely, unlimitedly surpassing—nature and the limited power of imaginal comprehension.

In the case of the dynamically sublime, the apprehensive moment is oriented to the excess of nature in the order of power. It is a matter of nature's superiority in power, its superiority to great hindrances (*Hindernisse*). How is such superiority to be judged, or, more precisely, how is it to be aesthetically estimated, apprehended? Kant's answer alludes to the reflective determination of the dynamically sublime in relation to practical reason; but also it outlines within the apprehensive moment a peculiar operation:

For in aesthetic judgment (without concept) superiority to hindrances can only be judged according to the greatness of the resistance. Now, that which we are impelled [*bestrebt sind*] to resist is, however, an evil [*Übel*], and, if we do not find our faculty [or capacity (*Vermögen*)] a match for it, an object of fear. Therefore, nature can be considered [*gelten*] by aesthetic judgment as power, and consequently as dynamically sublime, only insofar as it is regarded as an object of fear. [§ 28]

And yet, though nature is apprehended as exceedingly powerful only insofar as it appears as an object of fear, Kant insists that there could be no judgment of the sublime if overpowering nature were in a given instance actually to be feared. What is required, then, is that one regard the natural object as fearful without actually being afraid of it—that is, the apprehension must be such as to let the object appear fearful without, however, actually evoking fear. How is such an apprehension possible? By means of an operation removed from the actuality. In Kant's formulation, such apprehension of the fearful is possible "if we judge it in such a way that we merely think [*uns . . . denken*] the case in which we would want to resist it and yet in which all resistance would be altogether vain" (§ 28). It is a matter of thinking oneself into a state of fear before the fearful while still maintaining that reserve of distance that makes it possible not actually to be afraid of the fearful. More precisely, it is a matter not of thought in the strict sense but rather of an imaginal operation, a matter of "an attempt to place ourselves by imagination in that [state of fear]" (§ 29). It is a matter of supplementing the mere apprehension of the object with an imaginal enactment of resisting and being overpowered by the superior power of nature. It is a matter of an imaginal supplement to the mere apprehension of the object that one customarily (though improperly) calls dynamically sublime, a supplementary enactment that, in relation to such objects, would exhibit "our faculty [or capacity (*Vermögen*)] of resisting [as] insignificantly small in comparison with their power" (§ 28). Thus, in the judgment of the dynamically sublime too the apprehensive moment involves a certain experience of limitation, specifically, of the limitation of one's own power and, correlatively, of the excessive power of nature, of its unlimited capacity to overpower whatever resistance one might offer to it. It is an imaginally enacted experience in which, then, is disclosed the *difference* between an overpowering nature and the limited power of human resistance.

In both types of judgments of the sublime the apprehensive moment is thus found to issue in the disclosure of a certain difference. This disclosure is the site of the sublime, its site within experience, within the subject. The authentically sublime—in distinction from those objects commonly but improperly called sublime—is precisely the difference that comes to be disclosed at this site, the difference between nature and the sensible powers of man, imagination constituting the central yet complex element of the latter. This difference is what, in the further analysis, will prove to be purposive, harmonious, with respect to the faculties. Its disclosure, the opening of the difference, is what constitutes that movement of the mind that, in Kant's formulation, "is to be judged as subjectively purposive . . . and referred by the imagination either to the faculty of cognition or to the faculty of desire" (§ 24). And yet, precisely because it is movement, because it is an experience of radical excess, because it is a matter of difference, the site to which the sublime would now be withdrawn is not one at which the sublime would be delimited as a positive state within the subject. Rather, the authentically sublime is difference, the kinetic difference between man and nature.

Let me turn now to the central moment, the reflection in which this difference is referred to reason. Several passages will need to be examined in order to thematize this reflection at the appropriate level.

A global indication of the character of the reflection is given by the following passage, even though its formulation is oriented specifically to the mathematically sublime:

But because there is in our imagination a striving toward infinite progress [*ein Bestreben zum Fortschritte ins Unendliche*] but

in our reason a demand for absolute totality as a real idea,
therefore this very inadequation [*Unangemessenheit*] for that idea
in our faculty for estimating the magnitude of things of sense
is itself the awakening of a feeling of a supersensible faculty in
us. [§ 25]

Here Kant circumscribes the apprehensive moment as involving a striving toward infinite progress—that is, as striving to progress unlimitedly, as striving to extend without
limit the comprehension that would gather the sequence of
apprehensions. Precisely because it involves such a striving
to exceed all limits, imagination can encounter its limit and,
recoiling from it, experience its limitation in the face of the
excess of nature. But now, in the moment of reflection, it is
no longer the difference between imagination and nature that
is at issue; rather, the inadequation that comes to be exhibited, disclosed, in and through the reflection is one that
extends into another order. It is a matter of a disproportion, a
difference, between the rational idea, that is, the absolute
totality demanded by reason, and the limited comprehension
of which imagination is capable. The reflection refers imagination to reason—the imaginal order to the rational—in
such a way that a fundamental difference between them
comes to be disclosed.

There is need to press further with respect to several
questions broached by this global indication. If the reflection
issues in the disclosure of a fundamental difference between
imagination and reason, how exactly is this disclosure related
to that experience of limitation that is undergone in the
apprehensive moment? In other words, what exactly is the
character of the reflection that refers the apprehensively
disclosed difference between man and nature (the apprehensive difference) to the difference between imagination and
reason (the reflective difference)? And what is the agency of
this reflection? Finally, what is the character of the disclosure
in which the reflective difference comes to be exhibited? To
what faculty, what state of mind, is the difference displayed?

The question of agency is perhaps most directly answered,
in fact in a passage already cited in part in connection with

the apprehensive moment. Characterizing what is contained in that moment as a movement of the mind, in contrast to the restful contemplation characteristic of the judgment of taste, Kant writes of this movement that "it is referred by the imagination [*wird sie durch die Einbildungskraft . . . bezogen*] either to the faculty of cognition or to the faculty of desire" (§ 24). The reflection by which the movement of apprehension is referred to reason in those two capacities of the latter corresponding to the mathematically sublime and the dynamically sublime, respectively—this reflection is accomplished by imagination. But also imagination is involved in the movement of apprehension, involved not only in apprehension proper but more decisively and more freely in the comprehensive moment (in the case of the mathematically sublime) and in the supplementary enactment (in that of the dynamically sublime). Thus, one could say, with only minimal reservations, that the reflection is not only *by* imagination but also *of* imagination, that imagination refers itself to reason, that it is a matter of self-reflection.

But still more precision is needed regarding the terms of the reflection. The initial term, the terminus a quo, is what issues from the apprehensive phase. In the case of the mathematically sublime it is the experience of limitation, that is, an experience of the excess of nature, of its exceeding the imaginal capacity for comprehension, hence, an experience of the limit of that capacity. In short, it is a disclosure of the difference between unlimited nature and limited imagination, limited imaginal comprehension. In the case of the dynamically sublime the term is likewise a difference between nature and man, but in this case a difference within the order not of magnitude and imaginal comprehension of magnitude but of power and resistance; more precisely, it is a matter of the difference, disclosed through imaginal enactment, between overpowering nature and the limited power of human resistance. In both cases, then, what comes to be disclosed is the difference between nature and the sensible powers of man, these powers considered in the theoretical and the practical order, respectively.

What, then, of the final term of the reflection, its terminus ad quem? It too is a disclosure of difference but of a difference that extends into another order. In the case of the mathematically sublime it is the difference between man's limited capacity for imaginal comprehension and the unlimited demand of reason, its demand for the unlimited, the rational idea. In the case of the dynamically sublime it is the difference between man's limited capacity to resist, that is, his exposure to overpowering nature, and that superiority over nature that he enjoys as the gift of reason—in Kant's words, "a superiority over nature on which is grounded a self-preservation [*Selbsterhaltung*] of a kind entirely different from that which can be attacked and brought into danger by nature outside us" (§ 28). In both cases, then, what comes to be disclosed is the difference between man's limited sensible powers (as limited by nature) and his unlimited supersensible powers in the theoretical and the practical orders, respectively.

The reflection proceeds, then, from one difference to another, from the apprehensive difference to the reflective difference. What is the character of this reflective movement? How does it conjoin one difference to the other? How does it let one difference reflect the other?

Kant offers the following formulation: the natural object that is called (improperly, "by a certain subreption") sublime "renders intuitive [*anschaulich*] to us, as it were, the superiority of the rational determination of our cognitive faculties over the greatest faculty of sensibility" (§ 27). Another formulation refers to "ideas of reason, which, although no presentation [*Darstellung*] adequate to them is possible, are aroused and called to mind precisely through this inadequation that admits of sensible presentation" (§ 23). Hence, in the reflection it is a matter of rendering intuitive the superiority of reason over sensibility, over the greatest faculty of sensibility, which can only be imagination[10]; it is a matter of sensibly presenting the difference between reason and sensibility. In the apprehensive difference the reflective difference is sensibly presented, rendered intuitive.

There is a still more decisive formulation, which I extract now from a context that will have to be examined later: the reflection consists in a "straining [*Anspannung*] of imagination to use nature as a schema [*Schema*] for the latter [namely, the ideas]" (§ 29). It is a matter of exerting imagination to use nature as a schema for the ideas; or, as *Anspannung* also suggests, of a yoking of imagination, a harnessing of it (as of horses to a carriage or chariot). In other words, the reflection is a *schematizing*;[11] it consists in taking the difference between nature and the sensible powers of man as a schema for the difference between the sensible and the supersensible within man, letting the excess of nature, its exceeding of man's sensible powers, reflect the excess of reason, the superiority of the supersensible over the sensible. As in its central operation in theoretical cognition, so likewise, in its reflective operation in the judgment of the sublime, imagination is charged with a schematizing that conjoins reason and sense without reducing their difference; in the latter case, the conjunction issues in a disclosure within the sensible of the very difference between sensible and supersensible.

To what faculty, what state of mind, is this difference disclosed through the schematic reflection? Contrasting again the movement involved in the case of the sublime with the rest characteristic of the beautiful, Kant writes: "The mind feels itself moved [*fühlt sich . . . bewegt*] in the representation of the sublime in nature" (§ 27). It is moved not only in its recoil from exceeding nature but also in that disclosure that is accomplished through schematic reflection; and indeed it is preeminently in the latter case that feeling comes into play. Thus another passage:

Therefore, nature is here called sublime merely because it elevates the imagination to a presentation of those cases in which the mind can make felt to itself [literally, can make capable of being felt by itself (*sich fühlbar machen kann*)] the proper sublimity of its destination [or determination (*Bestimmung*)]. [§ 28]

Hence, it is to feeling that the disclosure accomplished by schematic reflection opens. Another passage formulates this result still more succinctly and even names the feeling that here comes into play:

The feeling of the inadequacy [*Das Gefühl der Unangemessenheit*] of our faculty for attaining to an idea that is law for us is respect [*Achtung*]. [§ 27]

This inadequacy, this inadequation, is precisely the difference that comes to be disclosed in reflection, the difference between man's limited sensible powers and his unlimited supersensible, rational, powers. This difference is felt; it is disclosed to feeling, to that feeling that Kant calls respect. Thus, as in the judgment of taste, so here too the moment of feeling proves to be, not something extrinsic to the judgment, not something merely produced by it, but rather an integral moment in its structure.

And yet, in the case of the sublime the feeling lacks that simplicity that is characteristic of the feeling within the judgment of taste. It lacks such simplicity, first of all, simply by virtue of being, in the first instance, a feeling of difference rather than of accord, harmony, unity; but its complexity lies especially in its division into two components, one component being that feeling of difference that has been outlined above, the other a feeling of unity conjoined, almost paradoxically, to the feeling of difference. This other component is expressed succinctly in the passage just cited, expressed in the phrase "law for us." The reference is to a law that would be purely rational and that would be also "for us," that is, binding upon man, a law to which he belongs in his very determination, a law by which he is, as it were, claimed, even if his sensible nature (his imaginal comprehension and his power of resistance) remains always inadequate to that law, falls short of it. In its full determination that law can of course only be the moral law, and this is why the feeling is called respect, the feeling in which both the separation of man's sensible nature from that law and the essential belonging to it are felt. For these two components correspond to the two moments of respect that are outlined in the analysis that the *Critique of Practical Reason* gives of this feeling engendered in the sensibly bound subject by the moral law.[12]

The twofoldness of the feeling of respect is a twofoldness of pleasure and pain:

The feeling of the sublime is therefore a feeling of pain arising from the inadequation between the aesthetic estimation of magnitude by the imagination and the estimation by reason; there is at the same time a pleasure thus excited, arising from the correspondence with rational ideas of this very judgment of inadequacy of our greatest faculty of sense, insofar as it is a law for us to strive after these ideas. [§ 27]

Kant stresses that the feeling of difference and the feeling of unity are interrelated moments, that of pleasure in unity being aroused, almost paradoxically, by that of pain in difference:

Therefore, the inner perception of the inadequacy of all sensible standards for rational estimation of magnitudes is a correspondence with rational laws; it involves a pain, which arouses in us the feeling of our supersensible destination, according to which it is purposive and therefore a pleasure to find every standard of sensibility inadequate to the ideas of reason. [§ 27]

The character of the purposiveness that proves finally to be displayed in the judgment of the sublime needs to be carefully examined. Almost from the outset it has been stressed that the natural object that is customarily called sublime is not properly so and that, correlatively, the purposiveness in the judgment of the sublime cannot lie in an accord of the object, as apprehended, with the faculties of the subject. For the character of such an object (most notably, the possibility of its being formless) is such as to preclude any such accord, that is, is such as to do violence to the imagination, exceeding it, escaping its comprehension (or, in the case of the dynamically sublime, is such as to threaten to overpower man's power of resistance). The purposiveness displayed in the judgment of the sublime is not, properly speaking, a purposiveness in nature. It is not in nature that a site is to be found for the sublime.

It appeared, then, that the sublime, withdrawn from nature, was drawn toward the subject, or, more precisely, into the space between subject and object. The sublime would occur at that limit defined by the experience of limitation, by the recoil of imagination from the excess of nature. The sublime would be that very movement at the limit, the movement in which is disclosed the difference between nature and man's sensible powers. In this case the purposiveness would—following the structure of reflective judgment in general—lie in the accord of this apprehensive difference with that to which it is referred in the reflection, the central moment of judgment. Thus, as the analysis of the reflection has now in effect shown, the purposiveness would lie in the accord between the apprehensive difference and the reflective difference, the latter consisting in the difference between man's limited sensible powers and his unlimited supersensible powers, preeminently between his imaginal and his rational powers. In a sense there is an accord between these two differences, and one could be tempted to identify this accord as the proper purposiveness of the judgment of the sublime; for the imagination is able to use the apprehensive difference as a schema for the reflective difference. And though there are passages in Kant's analysis that propose such an identification (presumably only as preliminary),[13] this is not the result to which that analysis finally leads. Schematism proves to be distinct from purposiveness, and that distinction is attested to by the feeling of pain that issues from the disclosure of the inadequacy of the sensible powers to what is demanded by reason; or, more precisely, it is attested to by the fact that the feeling to which the schematic disclosure opens is one of pain, whereas every disclosure of purposiveness opens to a feeling of pleasure. Why must the feeling attendant to the schematic disclosure be a feeling of pain? Because what is disclosed is not fundamentally an accord but rather a discord, that between the sensible and the supersensible in man.

And yet, finally a feeling of pleasure comes to attest to the purposiveness of the judgment of the sublime, a feeling of pleasure that is aroused by that very feeling of pain that attests to discord. How is it aroused? By the supervention of an accord, a purposiveness, upon the discord between the sensible and the supersensible. Yet the supervenient purposiveness does not eliminate the discord; it does not simply dissolve it but rather *is* precisely a purposiveness *of* that very discord. It is just such a purposiveness that is outlined in the two passages cited above (from § 27). In both passages the essential point is the same: the very disclosure of the discord, the discovery that every standard of sensibility is inadequate to the ideas of reason, the judgment of the inadequation of the greatest faculty of sense—such disclosure, discovery, judgment, is precisely in accord with reason. To find every standard of sensibility inadequate to the ideas of reason is precisely what is demanded by reason; such disclosure is in accord with reason; it is purposive and therefore is felt also with pleasure. It is a feeling of man's supersensible destination.[14]

The purposiveness displayed in the judgment of the sublime is thus displaced still further from nature. It is a purposiveness neither of the natural object nor even of the movement at the limit where the difference between man and nature is disclosed. Now it is a matter of coming to feel "a purposiveness quite independent of nature" (§ 23). The sublime is, then, still further withdrawn from the object, drawn back even from that limit at which man recoils from nature, drawn back now entirely into the subject: "We thus see also that true sublimity must be sought only in the mind of the one who judges . . ." (§ 26).

Where within the subject is the sublime now to be found? What is its new site? Or rather, what is the site that would finally be delimited for the sublime? That which can properly be called sublime is identified by Kant as "the disposition of spirit [*die Geistesstimmung*]" in which the judgment of the sublime issues (§ 25). But that disposition is simply the feeling in its finally pleasurable form, in Kant's words, "the feeling of a supersensible faculty in us" (§ 25). Thus it is no longer simply a matter of a feeling of purposiveness but of a feeling that is itself purposive. What is purposive, what is sublime, is that complex feeling to which is disclosed both the difference between sensible and supersensible and, in and through that very disclosure, man's essential orientation to the latter, his supersensible destination.

One cannot but notice in a few passages in the Analytic of the Sublime a tendency to draw the sublime even further, to delimit its site and bring its spacing finally under control by withdrawing it not only from the natural object but also from the natural, that is, sensible, subject. Thus: "The sublime is to be sought not in the things of nature but only in our ideas" (§ 25)—that is, not in a feeling of the ideas, not in the disclosure of them as man's essential destination, *but rather in the ideas themselves*. Or again: "The authentically sublime can be contained in no sensible form but concerns only ideas of reason" (§ 23). In this tendency one could suppose that a certain subreption is operative, a kind of analogue to that— which Kant has corrected—by which things of nature come to be called sublime. And yet, if the ideas are to be identified as the properly sublime, then the entire structure of the reflective judgment in relation to which the sublime was to have been understood will have been violated to an even greater degree, indeed completely. On the other hand, however, the sublime will have been drawn to a site where it can be decisively delimited, to the very site of delimitation as such.

Even without such a final step, the sublime comes to be assimilated to a classical opposition, in a sense the most classical one, the founding opposition of metaphysics. The sublime, withdrawn into the subject, becomes a feeling whose essential function is to disclose within man the opposition between sensible and supersensible while, in and through that very disclosure, orienting man toward the supersensible as his genuine destination. Thus, the sublime serves to disclose within man the field delimited by the opposition between sensible and supersensible, the field of metaphysics as such; and to disclose the essential orientation within that field, the orientation of the sensible toward the supersensible, the upward way of metaphysics. In the end, it discloses this field and this orientation not only within but also outside the subject; in a secondary reflection from the pure interiority of the sublime out upon nature, the latter too comes to be disclosed as oriented within the metaphysical field, though such disclosure is severely restricted, merely a matter of thought:

This striving—and the feeling of the unattainability of the ideas by the imagination—is itself a presentation of the subjective purposiveness of our mind in the employment of the imagination for its supersensible destination and forces us, subjectively, to *think* nature itself in its totality as a presentation of something supersensible [*als Darstellung von etwas Übersinnlichem*], without being able to establish this presentation *objectively*. [§ 29]

Both the interiority of the subject and the exteriority of nature come—with the necessary reservations—to be disclosed as oriented within the metaphysical field delimited by the opposition between sensible and supersensible. Most remarkably, this disclosure prescribes that imagination, however much it might have been freed from nature, must be held within bounds, limited, constrained; and it ordains, in this same connection, a repression of images in favor of that "merely negative presentation" of the supersensible that can be provided by the judgment of the sublime:

Perhaps there is no sublimer passage in the Jewish law than the command: Thou shalt not make to thyself any image nor any kind of likeness, neither of what is in heaven, nor of what is on earth, nor of what is beneath the earth, etc. . . . [W]here the senses see nothing more before them and the unmistakable and indelible idea of morality [*Sittlichkeit*] remains, it would be rather necessary to moderate [*mäßigen*] the impetus of an unlimited imagination, in order to prevent it from rising to enthusiasm, than, through fear of the powerlessness of these ideas, to seek aid for them in images and childish things. [§ 29]

It is hardly surprising, then, that in the development of the theory of the sublime one can discern, as with the judgment of taste, an erosion of the judgmental structure that Kant places initially at the center of the judgment of the sublime. As a reflective judgment, the judgment of the sublime would consist in the subsumption of a given particular under a universal that has to be sought out for it; but, as in the judgment of taste, the universal that proves to be involved is no universal in the usual sense but rather universality in the subject, that is, a cognitive faculty, namely, reason. Furthermore, at one level of the judgment of the sublime, the level in fact at which the judgmental structure as a whole remains most intact, the term that functions analogously to the sought-out universal is no positive term at all but rather the difference between reason and the sensible powers.

Just as in the judgment of taste, the reflection that forms the center of the judgment of the sublime proves to be an operation quite distinct from the subsumption—taken in a strongly cognitive sense—of a particular under a sought-out universal. Rather than being a cognitive-related operation that would supervene upon the otherwise aesthetic process, an additional faculty to be distinguished from reason and imagination, a faculty of judgment as such, the reflective operation proves instead to be an operation of imagination, specifically, one of schematizing, of using one kind of difference to present another. The judgment in the judgment of the sublime is as eroded, as effaced, as in the judgment of taste.

Indeed even more so. For not only do the universal term and the reflection into the universal diverge from what would be required by the structure of reflective judgment in that initial, strongly cognitive sense in which Kant takes it; but also, with the withdrawal of the sublime from the particular natural object, the other term too diverges, eroding the structure still further. Even at that level at which the judgmental structure remains most intact (a level that proves to be quite preliminary), the term that functions analogously to the particular is not a particular natural object but rather the movement at the limit, the recoil of imagination (or of imagined resistance) from exceeding nature, the kinetic difference between man and nature. When, in the development of the analysis, the sublime comes to be drawn entirely into the subject, the term that, from the point of view of the purposiveness involved, functions analogously to the particular turns out to be not that which is reflected (the apprehensive difference) but rather that which issues from the reflection, that to which the reflective disclosure opens, a feeling of pain through which is aroused a feeling of pleasure. In a sense of course a feeling, even one of such complexity, can be considered something particular. On the other hand, its initial intentionality compromises its particularity; it is a feeling not just of a difference, not just of a difference that is irreducible to particularity, but of the difference that opens the very distinction between universal and particular. If, finally, one were to follow that tendency found in some passages, the tendency to identify the sublime with the ideas themselves, then what would already be a violation of the structure of judgment would become its utter disruption.

d | Although the assimilation of the sublime to the metaphysical opposition between sensible and supersensible broaches a new appropriation of the aesthetic, the erosion of the judgmental structure in the judgment of the sublime has, as with the judgment of taste, the effect of strengthening that separation between the aesthetic and the cognitive (i.e., knowledge of particular objects) that was asserted in the Introduction to the *Critique of Judgment*. Setting aside for the moment the issue of the newly broached appropriation, let me focus on the question of the separation, now strengthened, between the aesthetic and the cognitive. Is this separation such that the judgment of the sublime (continuing to use this designation despite the erosion—hence, to a degree, writing it under erasure) simply has nothing to do with knowledge and truth? Or, on the other hand, is it only with knowledge and truth as customarily defined (and, for the most part, equated) that the judgment of the sublime has little or nothing to do—for instance, with knowledge as delimited in the *Critique of Pure Reason*? What of that complex feeling in which the judgment of the sublime issues? What about its disclosedness?

For indeed the entire analysis of the sublime has served to confirm that this feeling is disclosive, that it is not a mere "blind" feeling of pleasure and pain but rather is a state to which a certain disclosure opens, to which something comes to be revealed in a way that is irreducible, and ultimately incomparable, to theoretical knowledge (either as sensible intuition or as subsumption of such intuitions under concepts). The agency of the disclosure is indeed imagination, which is of course not without its role in the production of theoretical knowledge; but in the judgment of the sublime the schematizing operation of imagination not only is freed from the faculty that is legislative for theoretical knowledge, namely, understanding, but also is more thoroughly detached, more withdrawn, from the object than in the case of theoretical knowledge or even that of the judgment of taste. Furthermore, what is disclosed to such feeling is of course no object, nothing that could ever become an object of knowledge as defined in the *Critique of Pure Reason*. What is disclosed, in the first instance, is difference, the difference between reason and the sensible powers, the difference within man between the supersensible and the sensible. But then also there is disclosed man's essential orientation toward the supersensible, his true vocation, his proper destination.

The disclosure is thus preeminently a self-disclosure. In the judgment of the sublime one is disclosed to oneself in a way that is quite distinct from that exceedingly limited self-disclosure shown by critique to be the only form possible within theoretical knowledge, namely, the intuition of the self as it appears in inner sense. By contrast, the self-disclosure that takes place in the judgment of the sublime is an imaginal, affective reflection, irreducible to theoretical knowledge. But one could also draw the contrast in another way: in the judgment of the sublime the disclosure is not a matter of appearance, not a matter of bringing something to appearance, enticing it somehow to show itself; the disclosure is not a matter of bringing the self to light, as though it were a being previously enshrouded in darkness and upon which now light comes finally to shine. On the contrary, in the judgment of the sublime the self comes to be disclosed in that its essential space is disclosed, its proper field and the orientation within that field. That space, that field, is just the expanse delimited by the difference between supersensible and sensible, and the orientation is simply that prescribed by the sense of that opposition (if it is permissible to speak of the sense of that very opposition by which sense as such is delimited).

But there is another side to the disclosure that occurs in the judgment of the sublime, its natural side. For however much Kant's analysis stresses the withdrawal of the sublime into the subject, identifying it with the complex feeling of self-disclosure, it is not by sheer caprice that certain kinds of natural objects are customarily (if improperly) called sublime. And however withdrawn the truly sublime may be from such natural objects, there could be no judgment of the sublime without them. However inessential, however improper their sublimity, still they belong to the structure of the judgment of the sublime; or, more precisely, what belongs to that structure is the movement at the limit, the experience of limitation in which man recoils from exceeding nature. However complete the withdrawal into the subject, even into reason itself, this movement of difference at the level of apprehension cannot be excluded from the judgment of the sublime without simply and utterly eliminating sublimity as such.

It is usually to this movement that Kant refers when he contrasts the movement of the mind in the judgment of the sublime with the restful contemplation characteristic of the judgment of taste. In particular, it is to this movement that he refers in a passage in which he again tells how the mind is alternately attracted and repulsed and in which now he in effect names that movement by introducing the word *Erschütterung*, which I propose to translate by recourse to a fabrication that hovers between the isolation, the subject orientation, of *trembling* and the object orientation of *tremor*.

Here, then, is Kant's comparison of the movement of the mind with what I shall call *tremoring*:

> This movement can (especially in its beginning) be compared to a tremoring [*Erschütterung*], that is, to a rapidly alternating repulsion from, and attraction to the same object. That which is excessive [*das Überschwengliche*] for the imagination (up to which it is impelled in the apprehension of intuition) is, as it were, an abyss [*Abgrund*], in which it fears to lose itself; but for the rational idea of the supersensible [it is] not excessive [*nicht überschwenglich*] but lawful [*gesetzmäßig*] to bring forth such a striving of imagination, and consequently here there is the same amount of attraction as there was of repulsion for the mere sensibility. [§ 27]

The mind is thus shaken, a tremor comes over it, a state of trembling, pulsating, vibrating, that is not, however, confined to the subject but that is essentially linked up with an object, a natural thing, from which in a sense the tremoring spreads, comes over the subject, setting him moving. The movement is one of rapid alternation between being repulsed by the object and being attracted by that same object. What object? The object that is customarily (though improperly) called sublime, the object that, to take the case of the mathematically sublime, imagination strives to comprehend, only to reach a limit from which it recoils and at which the unlimitedness of nature, its exceeding of man's sensible powers, is disclosed. What produces the tremoring is the difference between the two appearances, the two guises, that this object can assume in relation to the judgment of the sublime. For imagination, for mere sensibility, it appears as *excessive*, as an *abyss* in which one fears losing oneself, as an unlimited, undelimitable space in which one could find no bearings. It appears thus as "the terrible [*das Abschreckende*]" (§ 29), and the subject is repulsed from it. For reason, on the other hand, neither the object nor imagination's striving to comprehend it appears as excessive. Rather than appearing as an excessive impulse toward an abyss, the striving of imagination now appears lawful, in accord with law, with the law of reason itself. The entire analysis of the judgment of the sublime, especially the withdrawal of the sublime into the subject, has served to demonstrate how this second appearance—and its correlative feeling of pleasure—arises. The point is that the reflection of the first appearance issues in a disclosure (to feeling) of the difference between reason and sensibility (within man), a difference the very disclosure of which is in accord with reason and arouses in man a feeling of his supersensible destination. Again it is a matter of a consequent, secondary reflection back upon nature, a reflection that constitutes the second appearance, canceling the appearance of excessiveness, referring the abyss (*Abgrund*) to ground as such, that is, reason. Now the natural thing becomes attractive, and the flight of imagination toward it no longer appears as a plunge into an abyss; now that flight appears not as an impulsive transgressing of limits but as one's essential rationality. This second appearance would be the truth that in the end would supervene, consigning the other appearance and hence the tremoring largely to the "beginning."

Kant outlines another alternation that corresponds quite precisely to that of the two appearances of the object. Now it is a matter of the violence produced by a certain suspension of time:

The measurement of a space (as apprehension) is at the same time a description of it, thus an objective movement in the imagination and a progression; on the other hand, the comprehension of the multiplicity [*Vielheit*] into unity—not of thought but of intuition—and thus the comprehension in a moment [*Augenblick*] of what is successively apprehended is a regression that suspends [*aufhebt*] the condition of time in the progression of imagination and makes *coexistence* intuitable. It is therefore (since the time series is a condition of inner sense and of an intuition) a subjective movement of imagination by which it does violence to inner sense, the more noticeable the greater the quantum is that imagination comprehends in one intuition. [§ 27]

On the one hand, imaginal comprehension, gathering into (a limited) unity what is successively, that is, at different times, apprehended, disrupts the condition of rigid temporal succession, suspends the condition of time; or rather, more precisely, it breaks free of complete subordination to temporal succession without, however, freeing itself entirely, for if it were to become entirely detached from temporal succession then it could not encounter that limit from which it recoils and from which the entire unfolding of the judgment of the sublime proceeds. But a limited break suffices to do violence to inner sense, to intuition, which is completely subordinate to temporal succession. To that extent imaginal comprehension produces a certain disordering of sensibility, an effect that could become terrible, abysmal. But, on the other hand, that effect, that violence, if reflected through the judgment of the sublime, serves precisely to disclose both the difference between reason and sensibility and man's essential orientation within that difference:

Thus that very violence that is done to the subject by imagination is judged as purposive *in reference to the whole determination* of the mind. [§ 27][15]

With respect to these alternations, these tremorings, a certain reflection through reason (primary and secondary reflection, from nature to reason and from reason, secondarily, back to nature), a certain circulation effected in the judgment of the sublime, plays a decisive role, the role of suppressing the alternation by finally exposing the excessive as lawful, the abyss as grounded, violence as purposive. Circulation through reason brings the tremorings to an end. But even before the end, even from the beginning, such circulation is already operative. Thus, in that passage at the beginning of the Analytic of the Sublime where Kant first introduces the judgment of the sublime as involving the representation of unlimitedness in a possibly formless object, he completes that very first account with a reference to reason, to a circulation through reason: "And yet its totality is added in thought" (§ 23). Again, in considering the mathematically sublime, he points in the same direction, toward the voice of reason: "But now the mind listens to the voice of reason, which, for every given magnitude, even those that can never be entirely apprehended . . . , demands totality" (§ 26). Several other passages indicate just how imperative it is that the circulation through reason be operative from the beginning. For example:

Thus the wide ocean, disturbed by storms, cannot be called sublime. Its look is horrible; and one must already have filled the mind with manifold ideas if it is to be disposed [*gestimmt*] by such an intuition to a feeling that is itself sublime. . . .
[§ 23]

Again, referring to the alternation between an appearance of terror that repulses and another appearance that attracts, Kant explains why the latter is attractive:

Because it is a dominion [*Gewalt*] that reason exercises over sensibility merely in order to extend it in conformity with its proper realm (the practical) and to let it look out to the infinite, which for it is an abyss [*Abgrund*]. In fact, without development of moral ideas, that which we, prepared by culture, call sublime presents itself to the unrefined man [*dem rohen Menschen*] merely as terrible [*abschreckend*]. [§ 29]

Tremoring, alternation between ground and abyss, between attraction and repulsion, between violating and uplifting the condition of time—this requires from the beginning that the circulation through reason be operative. That circulation does not, however, trace identical semicircles: what is primary is the gathering to reason, the gathering of reason, the withdrawal of the sublime from nature. This is why tremoring belongs "especially in its beginning," why the effect of the full judgment of the sublime is a new appropriation of the aesthetic, its appropriation to reason, its assimilation to cognition not in an empirical sense but in the most fundamental metaphysical sense. The aesthetic, the sublime, becomes another way of entering onto the upward way from sensible to supersensible.

From another perspective, one might say that, from the beginning and most fully at the end, the circulation through reason traces out a kind of guardrail that prevents one from slipping off into the excessive and disordered, that holds one back from the plunge into the terrible abyss. It is a guardrail that protects and preserves precisely that self-disclosure that is achieved in the judgment of the sublime. The circulation through reason prevents aesthetic self-disclosure from veering off into the abyss, draws it back into its alternation, into tremorings, and finally suppresses quite decisively the very possibility of the plunge, deciding, as it were, for the rational side, bringing everything essentially to rest there. The guardrail limits the spacing that commences as tremoring. It prevents one's ever decisively losing oneself in the abyss; it guarantees self-recovery, assures that self-disclosure is self-recovery.

But what if now—today—such assurance were no longer available? What if the guardrail were now displaced or even itself set in erratic motion? What if the circle that the judgment of the sublime would trace between reason and nature were decentered? What if the aesthetic circle were now eccentric with respect to what previously would have been called the circle of reason? Would such displacement have the effect of setting man adrift, of setting adrift even the determination of man as a sensible being possessing reason, as ζῷον λόγον ἔχον, the determination that is so thoroughly preserved in critique? Would it not set that being that has been called man adrift toward the excessive, the terrible, the abysmal? Would it not set him again tremoring and leave him bereft of any means of suppressing the drift, the tremorings? Would it not release the spacings that would have commenced as tremorings? Then the sublime would prove again to have withdrawn, not to a site that could be finally delimited for it, much less to the very site of delimitation as such, but rather into a certain drift away from delimitation, a drift between ground and abyss, a drift in which difference would be spaced out, a drift both exposed to the threat of a loss of self and open to the promise of ecstasy. One might want to call it a drift of abysmal imagination.

But what, then, about Carazan and his dream. Kant finishes the story by telling of how Carazan, in his bewilderment at being, in his dream, carried along beyond the limits of nature and on toward the immeasurable abyss—of how he finally thrust out his hand with such force toward the objects of reality that he awoke; and of how he then repented. Need it be said now that that other version of the story to which I have alluded would have to have a different ending? Or, perhaps, no ending at all.

5 | ENDING(S)—

Imagination, Presentation, Spirit

διὰ γὰρ τὸ θαυμάζειν οἱ ἄνθρωποι καὶ νῦν καὶ τὸ
πρῶτον ἤρξαντο φιλοσοφεῖν, . . .

[Aristotle, *Metaphysics* 982b]

Beginning on the periphery, which is to say not yet quite beginning, lingering there indecisively, neither within nor without. Wondering.

Can one imagine an eccentric beginning: (an) outside of spirit? Especially considering that the very form of being-outside, space as such, is only the *Aussersichsein* of that which is to be presented as spirit, also its *Ansichsein,* an outside already recoverable from the very beginning. Space will never have been outside, and spirit's being-outside-itself will never have been anything other than its being-present-to-itself. Any such beginning is utterly controlled by the end, is always already within the end of spirit. As soon as one begins, one is already at the end.

Is closure so utterly ineluctable? I wonder.

The figure must be still more eccentric, more disruptive.

Imagine, then, a spacing of closure that would exceed closure, that would perforate its covering, rending and riddling its sphere, opening it ever so minutely toward beginnings that would exceed the end, that would pluralize and defer it, endings.

With Hegel it is a matter of putting an end to wonder.

Hegel would reduce spacing, would temper its excess, moderating it into an operation within limits that, however fluid, would nonetheless remain secure. Within such security there could be only a question of placement, of placing every operation within the self-closure of spirit. There is no more rigorous reduction in the history of metaphysics; it is even the very concept of rigor thought through to the end. How could it, then, be rigorously undone, put seriously into question, except by reaching into the sphere and working from within, tracing the place of imagination in almost the same way as Hegel, with only the slightest eccentricity, the reserve of wonder.

a

My concern is, then, with the place of imagination in Hegel's philosophy of spirit.[1] More precisely, I want to examine the placing of imagination within presentation, to interrogate the way in which Hegel secures imagination within presentation. In this regard *presentation* is to be taken in at least three senses. These three senses can be discerned in the meanings that the words *Vorstellung, Darstellung,* and *Gegenwärtigung* have in reference to the Hegelian system. The first, expressed in *Vorstellung,* refers to a kind of activity of theoretical spirit, or rather, more precisely, to a certain range of development of theoretical spirit, a dialectical course stretching from intuition to thought. To ask about the place of imagination within presentation in this sense is to ask, as did Kant, how imagination mediates between intuition and thought. The second sense, expressed in *Darstellung,* is that according to which one would refer to the presentation of the system, for example, the presentation comprised by the philosophy of spirit.[2] To ask about the place of imagination in presentation in this sense is to broach the question of the agency of imagination in philosophical thought. It is to open an investigation that *could* lead one to conclude, as did Fichte, that imagination is the "faculty that determines whether one philosophizes with, or without, spirit."[3] And yet Hegel is not led to such a conclusion. He is not led to it primarily because of the way in which those senses of presentation expressed in *Vorstellung* and *Darstellung* are rigorously controlled by a third sense, the sense expressed in the word

Gegenwärtigung: presentation as making-present, bringing to presence, or, in the most relevant, reflexive form, bringing oneself to self-presence. Here the "one" of "oneself" is, in the end, spirit itself; and it is thus that Hegel thinks this sense of presentation through to its end, all coming to presence being sublated in the self-presentation of spirit, in absolute self-presentation. As such it gathers to itself not only that limited course of development that Hegel terms *Vorstellung* but also the very production of science itself, the presentation of the system.[4] If, beyond the Hegelian system, contemporary discussions have succeeded in showing that the position of presence (παρουσία, *Gegenwärtigkeit, Anwesenheit,* etc.) organizes the entire configuration of metaphysical thought, thus governing the entire history of philosophy, this only serves in a sense to confirm that Hegel did indeed think philosophy as such through to its end, that he brought it to its completion.

In focusing on the place of imagination in presentation in its manifold senses, I want, then, to show how Hegel thinks the problem of imagination through to its end. *End* is to be understood, first of all, in a historical sense. In this connection it is a matter of showing how Hegel's presentation of imagination in the philosophy of spirit brings to completion what was prepared from the beginning. Following Hegel's own directive, I shall deal only with Aristotle's theory of imagination, leaving open the question whether, from the standpoint of contemporary discussions, the Aristotelian theory can still be taken as exhaustive. It will be, then, a matter of showing how the essentials of Aristotle's theory of imagination are taken up by Hegel and brought to completion.

But *end* is to have here another sense too. According to this other sense it may be said that Hegel thinks imagination through to the point where, secured in its place within presentation (in all three senses), it is at an end as a problem, is no longer a problem, no longer provocative of questioning nor of the wonder with which, as both Hegel and Aristotle attest,[5] questioning begins. I shall want to raise a question about this appropriation of imagination to presentation, to ask about the securing of imagination within presence thought through to the end, to recall that imagination may have to do also with absence and withdrawal, perhaps in senses that are not merely complementary to presence and presentation.

b | Aristotle's theory of imagination (φαντασία) is presented in book 3 of his treatise *On the Soul*. Hegel's admiration for what Aristotle accomplished in this treatise is so profound that he regards Aristotle as virtually his only predecessor in the field dealt with in that treatise and the others related to it:

> Thus Aristotle's books on the soul, along with his dissertations on its special aspects and conditions, are still by far the best or even the sole work of speculative interest on this general topic. The essential purpose of a philosophy of spirit can be none other than reintroducing the concept into the cognition of spirit and so reinterpreting the meaning of these Aristotelian books. [*Enz.* § 378]

In the Kehler manuscript, which consists of student's notes on Hegel's lectures of 1825 on the philosophy of spirit, there is a similar testimony:

> The best that has been said of spirit has been said by Aristotle, and if one wants to know spirit speculatively one has only to consult him.[6]

This statement is followed by a series of quotations in Greek from the treatise *On the Soul*.[7]

Let me, then, following Hegel, turn to the Aristotelian treatise, to the discussion of imagination in book 3, chapter 3 (427 a 17–429 a 10). For the sake of conciseness—though at the cost of passing over many of the complexities of Aristotle's text—let me attempt to formulate Aristotle's theory of imagination in a series of six theses.

The first thesis expresses something that is determined by

Aristotle's very placing of imagination, by his assigning to the investigation of imagination a place within the treatise *On the Soul*. Imagination belongs to the soul, is a part of the soul. More precisely, it is a power or faculty of the soul (δύναμις τῆς ψυχῆς).

The second thesis assigns to imagination a place within the soul. Aristotle writes: "For imagination is different from both sensation [αἴσθησις] and thought [διάνοια]; imagination does not occur without sensation, nor judgment [ὑπόληψις] without it."[8] The place is thus intermediate. Imagination is an intermediate faculty of the soul.

The third thesis links this intermediate power of the soul to images. Aristotle writes: "Imagination [φαντασία] is that by which an image [φάντασμα] occurs for us." To draw out the subtlety at which Aristotle's statement only hints, imagination is that faculty by which an image not only is born (γίγνεσθαι) but therein comes to be *for us* (ἡμῖν).[9]

But, according to Aristotle, imagination can have to do not only with one image but with many, or rather, with making one out of many. Aristotle writes: "Hence we have the power of making a single image out of a number of images." This is, then, the fourth thesis. It broaches—though not so centrally as it will come to be by Hegel's immediate predecessors—the character of imagination as power of synthesis.[10]

The fifth thesis specifies the relation of imagination to sensation. Aristotle submits that the process of sensation involves a kind of movement (κίνησις) brought about by the actual operation (ἐνέργεια) of sensation and similar to that sensation. In addition to this movement of sensation, there is, then, imagination, itself also a kind of movement. To cite a few words extracted from Aristotle's very complex formulation: "Imagination appears to be some kind of movement and not to occur without sensation." He concludes: "Imagination must be a movement produced by sensation in actual operation."[11] The process of sensation—sensing or, as one might better say, perception or sense-intuition—is a movement brought about by the actual operation of sensation. Imagination is, then, another movement, a secondary movement generated from, if not simply by, the movement of sense.[12]

And yet, however much generated by the movement of sensation, imagination is in a significant regard a movement in precisely the opposite direction, a movement that, instead of drawing the soul toward things, involves a decisive withdrawal from them. The sixth thesis attributes to imagination this directionality and distance from what is present. Without ever quite formulating it explicitly, Aristotle develops it by means of a series of contrasts of imagination with other powers. Opinion, he observes, lacks detachment; in his words, "it is not in our power to form opinions as we want"—that is, we form opinions (δοξάζειν) in view of how things seem (δοκεῖν) to us.[13] By contrast, writes Aristotle, "in imagination we are like spectators looking at something dreadful or encouraging in a picture."[14] Aristotle extends the contrast to include knowledge (ἐπιστήμη), intelligence (νοῦς), and of course sensation. In these instances there is even less detachment than in the forming of opinions. The index of such detachment is the capacity to be false, that is, the power not to be simply bound by what is present. Thus Aristotle writes: "All sensations are true, but most imaginations are false. . . . Nor is imagination any one of the faculties that are always true, such as knowledge or intelligence; for imagination may be false." Thus marking the detachment of imagination from what is present, Aristotle also indicates, on the other side, the distinctive connection of imagination with absence—writing, for example: "Visions are seen by men even with their eyes shut." Still further, Aristotle refers to another moment of detachment at a quite different level, a detachment from its own being-present: "Sensation is always present [ἀεὶ πάρεστι] but imagination is not." This is, then, the sixth thesis: the detachment of imagination from presence.

With this thesis a space is opened between imagination

and presentation. It will be especially important to observe
how Hegel elaborates that openness while at the same time
sublating it in the comprehensive closure of spirit.

c | In the Hegelian system imagination belongs to spirit, is one
of the activities of spirit. Without entering systematically
into Hegel's discussions of spirit in general, let me simply
note two determinations that are important for the issues to
be raised with regard to imagination. I shall not attempt to
mark at all the limits of these two determinations. The first is
introduced through the discussion of spirit as sublating the
externality of nature:

> All the activities of spirit are nothing but various ways in
> which that which is external is led back to internality, to what
> spirit is itself, and it is only by means of this leading back,
> this idealizing or assimilation of that which is external, that
> spirit becomes and is spirit. [*Enz.* § 381 *Zusatz*]

In particular, then, imagination will be a way by which
externality is assimilated to internality. The second determination pertains to the capacity of spirit to endure the pain
of such assimilation. The formal essence of spirit is determined as freedom, the absolute negativity of the concept as
self-identity. Hegel explains:

> In accord with this formal determination, spirit *can* abstract
> from all that is external and even from its own externality, its
> determinate being. It can endure the negation of its individual
> immediacy, the infinite pain, that is, in this negativity it can
> maintain itself affirmatively and be identically for itself. [*Enz.*
> § 382]

Thus, spirit's endurance is such that it can survive all dis-
memberment, reemerging from its loss of self into a reaffirmation of its self-identity, indeed an affirmation that is richer
as a result of the loss, that therefore is never, in the end, pure
loss. Hegel will think imagination through to the end in the
sense not only of filling out and completing the Aristotelian
account but also of thinking it through to that point at which

what was lost is recovered, to that end in which negativity comes to serve for reaffirmation, difference for self-identity, and absence for the recovery of presence.

Let me now narrow the focus to subjective spirit, the first, ideal moment in the development of spirit; and, still further, to the third moment within subjective spirit, the moment entitled simply "spirit" and designated as the subject of psychology. Though in fact several discussions pertaining to imagination are found in earlier stages, most notably in the anthropology (e.g., in *Enz.* § 408 *Zusatz*), it is within psychological spirit that imagination has, for Hegel, its place. Indeed, it will prove to be so secured to this place that the traces that it leaves behind in the anthropology will eventually become problematic.

Spirit, the subject of psychology, is the truth, the unity, of the first two moments in the development of subjective spirit. Like the second moment, consciousness, it stands as one side over against an object; and yet, like the first moment, the soul, it is also both sides and therefore a totality, not because, as with the soul, it fails to make the distinction of self from object, but because it has sublated that distinction. This result is expressed by saying that spirit is reason, the identity of subjective and objective. And yet, initially, in its immediacy, Hegel says,

Spirit is only the indeterminate certainty of reason, of the unity of the subjective and the objective. That is why at this juncture it still lacks determinate cognition of the rationality of the object. In order to attain it, spirit has to liberate the implicitly [*an sich*] rational object from the form of contingency, singularity, and externality that clings to it in the first instance, and so free itself from being related to something other than itself. [*Enz.* § 441 *Zusatz*]

The various faculties of spirit with which psychology deals can be treated in a rational way only if they are regarded as stages in this liberating of spirit to itself. Imagination will prove to be one of the ways, one of the stages, in this self-liberation of spirit.

Let me narrow the focus still more so as to determine more

specifically the place of imagination. That place lies within the first of the three moments of spirit, the moment of theoretical spirit. At this stage spirit involves a double determination: it both finds something within itself as a being and, on the other hand, posits it only as its own. Theoretical spirit, which Hegel also calls intelligence, is the transition from the first of these determinations to the second; that is, it is the activity by which the seemingly alien object comes by degrees to be assimilated,[15] by which spirit comes to posit the immediate affection as its own. Finding itself immediately determined, theoretical spirit comes to posit that determination as its own.[16] The course followed by such knowledge—or, more specifically, by what could be called cognition, thus translating *Erkennen,* which Hegel at this point distinguishes from *Wissen*—this course is described by Hegel as "a conceptually determined, necessary transition from one determination of intelligent activity (a so-called faculty of spirit [*Vermögen des Geistes*]) to another" (*Enz.* § 445). Imagination is, for Hegel as for Aristotle, one of these faculties and thus constitutes one stretch on the course of theoretical spirit.[17]

Anticipating this course, Hegel cautions against a certain way of regarding the faculties, namely, that in which each faculty is regarded as a fixed, independent determinateness and spirit therefore as a mere collection of isolated faculties. A similar caution is found in Aristotle (cf. 432 a–b); also, Hegel suggests, a similar attempt to deal with the soul in terms of a series of progressive determinations, even though the attempt remained incomplete and the determinations were not entirely blended into a whole.[18]

Hegel formulates the issue also in terms of the relation between the activity proper to spirit, namely, cognition, and the various faculties or activities that are ascribed to spirit. In saying that intelligence cognizes, it is not to be understood that, along with its cognizing, intelligence also intuits, presents, imagines, etc. Rather, cognition is the actuality of spirit, and intuiting, presenting, imagining, etc. are simply moments of this actualization. Hegel explains regarding cognition:

> The moments of its realizing activity are intuiting, presenting, recollecting, etc.; the activities having no other immanent significance; their only end [*Zweck*] being the concept of cognition. It is only when they are isolated that they are presented as being useful for something other than cognition, as affording cognitive satisfaction by themselves, so that a fuss is made about the delights of intuition, recollection, phantasy, etc. [*Enz.* § 445]

On the other hand, Hegel grants that even isolated intuiting, imagining, etc. can afford a certain kind of satisfaction. And yet, having granted such diversion, he displaces it from the truth:

> It will be admitted, however, that *true satisfaction* is afforded only by an intuiting pervaded by understanding and spirit, by rational presentation, by productions of phantasy, etc. pervaded by reason, exhibiting ideas, that is, by cognitive intuiting, presenting, etc.

But will it be, must it be, admitted? Can imagining provide *true* satisfaction only insofar as it is pervaded by reason, only insofar as it serves the end of cognition, serves for spirit's coming to be present to itself in what initially seemed an alien object? Can imagination provide *true* satisfaction only by serving self-presentation? And even if so, must it be admitted that truth is the sole measure of satisfaction? Could one not ask, for instance, about that intrinsic connection, stressed by Aristotle, between imagination and falsity? Could one not wonder about the very appropriateness of truth as a measure of imagination?

Within theoretical spirit, presentation is the middle term, stretching between intuition and thought. Imagination, placed within presentation, will be, as with Aristotle, an intermediate faculty. Intuition, the first moment of theoretical spirit, has an immediate object; or rather it is the movement of coming to have such an object. Beginning as sensation of the immediate material, that is, as feeling, it passes through the diremption brought by attention, which both fixes the object and separates that object from itself; and thus it comes to posit the object as self-external, to project it into the forms of space and time (cf. *Enz.* §§ 445 *Zusatz*, 446–48). The movement of presentation, beginning at this point, will be brought to completion at the stage of thought where the immediate, implicit unity present in intuition will be restored out of the oppositions that will have arisen intermediately, in the movement of presentation. Beginning at that point at which the movement of intuition ends, presentation—hence also imagination—is, as in Aristotle, a secondary movement generated from the movement of intuition, of sensation. And in the transition to thought, in the restoration of the unity that will have been disrupted, presentation—hence also imagination—will be thought through to the end.

Hegel outlines the course of presentation quite precisely:

> The course taken by intelligence in presentations is to render the immediacy internal, to posit itself as intuiting inwardly [*in sich selbst*], while to the same extent sublating the subjectivity of inwardness, and so in itself externalizing that which pertains to it that it is in itself in its own externality. [*Enz.* § 451]

As in intuition, there is a double movement, one directed inwardly, the other outwardly. But in the case of presentation the movements are not simple positings of internal and external in their opposition but rather a positing of external as internal and of internal as external. More specifically, it is a matter of internalizing the intuition while also in a sense positing in external form, as an outward double, what has been internalized.

At the threshold of presentation Hegel cautions again against taking the various forms of spirit to be independent faculties instead of grasping the rational connections between them and recognizing the sequence as the development of intelligence. At the standpoint of presentation there is, Hegel remarks, an even greater tendency than in previous stages to be diverted into such an ultimately irrational approach.

Within presentation, imagination is the middle term, stretching between recollection (*Erinnerung*) and memory (*Gedächtnis*). Recollection,[19] the first stage of presentation, is the moment of internalizing—that is, spirit's collecting, its gathering, to itself what has been yielded by intuition, its positing as its own a content now isolated from the external space and time of intuition, now deposited within spirit's own space and time. Though this content remains the same as in intuition, it now has the form, not of intuition, but of *image* (*Bild*) (*Enz.* § 452). Hence, in recollection, at the threshold of imagination, the image is born within us, even though it is only in imagination proper that it will become, in Hegel's sense, *for us*. Again it is an Aristotelian thesis that is being thought through to the end.

But the birth of image from intuition is only the first moment of recollection. Recollected within intelligence, transposed into the space and time of intelligence and the corresponding implicitness, the image is, Hegel says, "no longer existent but is *preserved* unconsciously" (*Enz.* § 453). Intelligence is thus "a nocturnal pit [*Schacht*] within which a world of infinitely many images and presentations is preserved without being in consciousness." But then, such images, slumbering within the nocturnal pit, can be recollected from the depths and brought into the light of determinate existence only through relation to an intuition. The third moment of recollection introduces therefore a certain movement of externalization, and what is properly called recollection is precisely the relating of the image to an intuition:

The images of the past lying latent in the dark depth of our inner being become our *actual possession* in that they come before intelligence in the bright, plastic shape of an intuition, a *determinate being* of *equivalent* content, and we, helped by the *presence* of this intuition, recognize them as intuitions we have already had. [*Enz.* § 454 *Zusatz*]

The image, thus called up from the pit by the intuition in such a way as to be separated from both pit and intuition, has come to be presented as image. This separation and the transition to imagination that it prepares mark the birth of the image *for us*.

Let me, then, finally narrow the focus to imagination itself. Hegel's treatment of it occurs in sections 455–59 of the *Encyclopedia,* section 460 providing then the transition to memory. Of the five sections devoted to imagination, all but one involve a supplementary remark by Hegel, amplifying the more concise statement in the section proper. All but one of the five sections also include *Zusätze* added to the text by Boumann in his 1845 edition of the 1830 version of the *Encyclopedia* and based on two of Hegel's notebooks as well as five sets of notes on Hegel's lectures.[20] Especially in the final section, where the discussion turns to language, the supplementary remark as well as the *Zusatz* are extended quite out of proportion to the section proper and to the remarks and *Zusätze* to most other sections of the *Encyclopedia*. I shall have to forgo giving attention to this extended final section. The other sections must, however, be considered with some care and with attention to the difference between Hegel's own text and the *Zusätze*.

In section 455 Hegel considers the first form of imagination. He terms it "reproductive imagination" and identifies it as "the issuing forth [*Hervorgehen*][21] of images from the ego's own inwardness." The reference is to the pit from which, in the final stage of recollection, images were called forth by intuitions.

The *Zusatz* to section 455 proceeds to outline quite distinctly the development of imagination even beyond this first form; in fact, it outlines the entire course of imagination right up to the transition to memory. Defining imagination in general as that which determines images, it proceeds to describe the three forms of imagination as three different ways in which images come to be determined. The first way is that of reproductive imagination, already identified in the section proper as the first form of imagination. In this case the determining consists in drawing images from the nocturnal pit out into determinate existence. The *Zusatz* adds something that, though briefly mentioned at the end of the final section on recollection, is not entirely explicit in section 455 proper: that with the transition from recollection to imagination, the reproduction, the issuing forth of images from the pit, comes to occur voluntarily and without the aid of a corresponding intuition.[22]

The second form of imagination is, according to the *Zusatz,* associative imagination, which relates images to one another and in that way elevates them to universality. Thus in associative imagination that power comes into play that is expressed in another of the Aristotelian theses, that which ascribes to imagination the power of making one out of many, of bringing many images into a one. It is noteworthy, however, that the one is not itself simply another image but rather is a representation elevated to the level of universality, thus directing the course of imagination toward an end in which the image will finally be sublated and imagination itself thought through to the end.

The third form of imagination enumerated in the *Zusatz* to section 455 is phantasy. In this instance the universal presentation resulting from the previous form is what gets determined by imagination. Specifically, it gets determined as having over against itself a determinate being in which it is imaged and with which in that sense it is identical. This determinate being can assume two forms, that of symbol and that of sign; and so, the third stage of imagination consists of two types of phantasy, symbolic phantasy and sign-making phantasy.

Such is, then, the outline provided by the *Zusatz* to section 455. It is important to observe, however, that in section 455 itself Hegel does not venture nearly so far. Having identified reproductive imagination as the first form, he proceeds only to mention that there is a certain content deriving from spirit, set forth out of the pit, and providing a "general presentation for the associative relation of images." The supplementary remark following the section proper is largely devoted to criticism of certain views concerning association of ideas, and there is—quite remarkably—no mention of associative imagination as a second form of imagination in general.

In fact, in section 456 associative imagination appears to be rather merely the transition to the second form. For association is "also to be grasped as a *subsumption* of singulars under a universal that constitutes their connection."[23] A difference is thus introduced between image and universality; and yet insofar as the universality comes to have a content derived not just from the stock of images but from intelligence itself as determinate concrete subjectivity, the movement between these moments becomes a recollecting of self by way of an imaging of intelligence back to itself.

Consequently it is inwardly and determinately recollected in this stock and informs [*einbilden*] the latter with its content—it is thus phantasy, the symbolizing, allegorizing, or poetical imagination.

This form of imagination constituted in the movement of imaginal recollection, namely, phantasy, Hegel explicitly marks as the second form of imagination.

It appears that Hegel may have labored over this transition, specifically over the transition that the universal undergoes, since its presentation was thoroughly revised in the 1827 edition and again in 1830. In certain respects it is most directly expressed in the 1827 version:

Initially, this universality is the form of intelligence, and the *content* of the subsuming presentation belongs to what is found [*dem Vorgefundenen*]. Intelligence, however, (taken anticipatively) as *in itself determinate* subjectivity, has its own content, which can be thought, concept, or idea.

It is, then, a matter of the images coming to be subsumed under the latter rather than the former content, a matter of a shift in the content of the operative universality. There is one quite significant indication that is missing in the 1817 edition, added in parentheses in 1827, and then expanded (without parentheses) in 1830, namely, the indication that this transition involves a certain exceptional anticipation of determinations of spirit far in advance of the form here being presented.[24] To the degree that such an anticipation is operative, the character of the development as a thinking of imagination to the end becomes still more prominent.

The lack of correspondence between Hegel's own text and the *Zusatz* to section 455 is now explicit. According to Hegel's text, reproductive imagination is the first form and phantasy the second; associative imagination, to the extent that one can consider it a distinct form, constitutes at most the transition from reproductive imagination to phantasy. The *Zusatz*, on the other hand, fixing associative imagination as the second form, displaces phantasy (specified as symbolic) into the third phase of imagination, compounding it with the form that Hegel's own text will place there. Though the significance of such enumeration clearly has its limits, especially given Hegel's strictures against isolating the forms of presentation as independent faculties, still these forms can be considered as stages in a development only if they are delimited; the enumeration belongs to that delimitation, and to this extent the confusion introduced by the apparent disorder in the *Zusatz* is a matter of serious concern.

Hegel's enumeration of the forms of imagination is somewhat more distinct within the simpler structure of the first edition, in which the treatment of imagination consists of three sections. In the second of these sections (§ 377), which corresponds to and to some degree is identical with section 456 in the later editions, Hegel refers to the association of presentations—not to the associative imagination—but then introduces phantasy in such a way as to suggest quite strongly that it is to be considered the second form. On the other hand, in Hegel's lecture notes to section 376 (corresponding to § 455 in the later editions) the following enumeration is found: "α) reprod[uctive] β) associirende—subj-[ectiv] auflösend allgemeine γ) symbolisirend."[25] But it is not clear whether this is to be taken as an enumeration of the forms of imagination—the absence of sign-making phantasy would dictate against this supposition—or as merely tracing the movement from reproductive imagination to phantasy via association.

It is of course possible that the lack of correspondence between the enumeration in Hegel's own text and in the *Zusätze* reflects a certain development. In composing the *Zusätze* Boumann conflated the difference between notes based on several different lecture courses dating from 1817 up to 1830; and by his own testimony he gave "the comparatively raw material of these lectures the artistic form justifiably required of a scientific work."[26] Such a manner of composing could have resulted in covering over, yet retaining a trace of, a development in Hegel's way of presenting imagination. The problem is especially acute because it is virtually impossible now to analyze Boumann's editorial work, most of the notes he used being no longer available.[27]

But, quite aside from the *Zusätze* and all the problems they raise, there is still another variation, another enumeration different from that given in Hegel's text proper. It is found in two unpublished transcriptions of lectures by Hegel on subjective spirit: Hotho's transcription of the lectures of 1822 and Griesheim's of those of 1825. The two transcriptions present essentially the same enumeration. The first form of imagination is the reproductive. The second, however, is neither simply associative imagination nor phantasy but rather that form that, especially in the Griesheim transcription, is carefully differentiated from association, namely, that determining that brings into play the distinction between universal and particular; in the Hotho transcription it is called "the process of making presentation universal [*das zum Allgemeinenmachen d{er} Vorstellung*]." The third form is, then, phantasy, "in which the universal presentation and the images are connected [*in d{er} allg{emeine} Vorstellung u{nd} d{ie} Bilder verbunden sind*]."[28]

For the present, at least, there is insufficient textual basis for resolving these differences. Nor is the textual basis sufficient for venturing, for instance, the suggestion that the disorder may stem from the matter itself. To suggest on the basis of the matter itself that there may be some disordering intrinsic to imagination would, of course, be something quite different.

Having marked these textual problems, let me continue. The *Zusatz* to section 456 begins by stressing the dependence of the universalizing operation on intelligence; universality could never arise by mere superimposition of similar images. However, the most important contribution of this *Zusatz* is the way in which it assembles the moments of phantasy into that movement as a whole. As a result of the role of intelligence in the generation of universality, the opposition between image and universal assumes within the present form the character of an opposition between internality and externality, which is then brought to unity as imaginal recollection, as the conjunction of an imaging of the universal with a universalizing of the image. And yet, this unity is no mere conjunction, no mere neutral product. Rather, the unity proceeds from the side of internality, from the activity of intelligence as the element of universality, proceeds, as the *Zusatz* expresses it,

> by its activating and proving itself as the substantial power over the image, subjugating the image, making itself the soul of the image, coming to be for itself, recollecting itself, manifesting itself, in the image. In that intelligence brings forth this unity . . . , the presenting activity, insofar as it is the *productive imagination*, completes itself internally.

This unity of internality and externality, this phantastical unity on the side of internality, constitutes the formal element of art, which, though at the level of absolute spirit, presents the universal in the image.

The *Zusatz*, though indeed amplifying the account of phantasy in section 456 proper, at the same time introduces a designation that does not occur in Hegel's own text, namely, *productive imagination*. It is not clear how it relates to the enumeration given in the previous *Zusatz*, much less to that in Hegel's text proper. Is it simply to be equated with phantasy (in the sense specific to § 456)? Or is it, as productive, to be contrasted with reproductive imagination and hence extended to cover all other forms? Is intelligence not productive in the generation of universality from the stock of images? Is it not productive especially in that third form of imagination that Hegel is about to introduce, that form in which occurs the making of signs?[29]

Section 457 introduces the third form of imagination as constituted by an addition to the subjective self-intuition achieved in phantasy, by the addition of the moment of being. It is a matter of a movement of externalization by which that in which phantasy is imaged back to itself, the stock of images, comes to be determined *as being*. This occurs in what Hegel's text proper marks explicitly as the third form of imagination: sign-making phantasy (*Zeichen machende Phantasie*). Hegel's Supplementary Remark adds a clarification: "The image produced by phantasy is only subjectively intuitable. In the sign, phantasy adds proper intuitability."

The *Zusatz* to section 457 is especially instructive in that it elaborates the character of that phantasy that Hegel's text enumerates as constituting the second form of imagination, distinguishing it, as symbolic phantasy, from the sign-making phantasy to which section 457 has just moved, and clarifying therefore that move. According to the *Zusatz*, symbolic phantasy is distinguished from sign-making phantasy by the fact that in it intelligence still pays heed to the given content of the images:

In order to express its universal presentations, this phantasy selects only that sensuous material that has an *independent* significance *corresponding* to the specific content of the universal to be imaged. The strength of Jupiter, for example, is represented by the eagle, since the eagle is supposed to be strong.

Much the same can be said of allegorical and of poetic phantasy, that is, of all phantasy prior (at least in certain of its moments) to the inception of signs. This inception replaces the imaginal attestation of universality with an objective attestation:

Now in that the universal presentation liberated from the content of the image makes itself into something intuitable within
an external material *voluntarily* selected by itself, it brings forth
what has to be called—as specifically distinct from a symbol—
a *sign*.

As Hegel himself expresses it—symbolically—in section
458 (Rem.):

The *sign* is a certain immediate intuition, presenting a content
that is wholly distinct from that which it has for itself;—the
pyramid in which an alien soul is displaced and preserved.

In the transition to the final form of imagination it is,
then, a matter of canceling the internality, the subjectivity,
that still belonged to that self-intuition constituted by the
circuit of image and universal or of symbol and intelligence.
To cancel that subjectivity requires that that in which intelligence intuits itself be no longer an image appropriated to
subjectivity but rather an objective being, a being that
remains objective, unappropriated, even as functioning to
present spirit to itself. Hegel can thus write that phantasy—
that is, sign-making phantasy—"is the central point in
which the universal and being, one's own and what is merely
found [*das Eigene und das Gefundensein*], the inner and the
outer, are made completely one." And it is thus that he can
write, even if with qualifications, that "phantasy is reason"
(§ 457 Rem.).

d   If one could, even momentarily, withdraw from the incessant
movement of presentation, if one could somehow detach
oneself, then one might indeed wonder at this result, that
phantasy is reason. One might wonder that the loss of self in
phantasy comes thus to be recovered. One might wonder that
the displacement of self into the play of images serves so
entirely in the end to lead the self back to its proper place, to
recover its presence.

Let me venture, then, a question. The question might

read: Does phantasy exceed reason? Or, more generally, is imagination in excess of spirit? The question is difficult—excessively difficult—to sustain. The difficulty lies in the necessity of not understanding excess here in that sense that would be operative if one were to say, with Hegel—and as he in effect says—that reason exceeds phantasy, that it is a more central central-point. It is a matter of attempting to think excess nondialectically, or rather—since this very formulation can so easily become dialectical—to think it in excess of dialectic.

Let me venture, then, this question of excessive imagination. Let me venture it, not in order to move on as economically as possible to an answer by which the interrogative loss of assurance would thus be recovered. Let me rather insist on the question, persist—even if only momentarily—in attempting to learn how, if at all, it can be asked with sustenance.

Along the way up to and through Hegel's presentation of imagination, I have marked those moments in which the various theses composing Aristotle's theory of imagination are taken up and thought through. Thus imagination is for Hegel a faculty of spirit, as it was for Aristotle a faculty of the soul; and Hegel, resuming an Aristotelian tendency, prohibits regarding imagination or any other faculty as something fixed and independent. It is of utmost consequence that what generates this prohibition is the demand that imagination (and all other faculties) be rigorously subordinated to cognition, that it be placed within presentation, retained in the service of absolute presentation. Thus placed, imagination is, then, as for Aristotle, an *intermediate* faculty; but that intermediate character is now thought through to the end, thought as mediation operating in spirit's discovery and recovery of itself in the image. As such, imagination belongs, as in Aristotle, to a secondary movement generated from the movement of intuition or sensation, a secondary movement that—for Hegel, thinking it to the end—resumes that movement of self-recovery that it was the function of intuition to begin. That resumption is broached by recollection, which gives birth to the image and recalls it from the nocturnal pit, letting it be reborn *for us*. Taking over the manifold of images, imagination proper then exercises that power that Aristotle ascribes to it, the power of making one out of many images. And yet, the one is not an image but a one thought through to the end. Even in its more developed forms, as phantasy, imagination remains a certain drawing of the many back to the one—as indeed it must if it is to remain in service to self-presentation.

But what about the final Aristotelian thesis? What about the detachment of imagination from presence? Clearly Hegel also resumes this thesis: one could say that the entire movement of recollection leading up to reproductive imagination is precisely a matter of intelligence's detaching itself from the immediate presence of the intuition; and one might also say that the transition to sign-making phantasy is a matter of detachment from presence in the form of the image or symbol. However, the question—the question I want to venture—is not simply whether there is such a detachment operative in imagination but rather whether that detachment disrupts to the end or only serves to prepare a new attachment, a new assimilation. The question is whether imagination can detach itself from presence so disruptively as to exceed being regathered into the circle of self-presentation. Can imagination be so disruptively detached as to be in excess of spirit?

In a certain sense it is perfectly obvious, as Hegel fully recognized, that there are certain forms of imagination that are quite disruptively detached, forms of imagination that break out of the movement of self-presentation, stationing themselves outside its periphery. What is especially noteworthy is the strategy that Hegel adopts in order, in a sense, to grant these forms their externality while insuring that they pose no threat to the integrity of self-preservation. The strategy is one of systematic displacement and consequent repression. Certain forms of imagination are displaced from psychology to anthropology, to a phase where, as a result of the element of corporeality that still remains undetached from spirituality (*Geistigkeit*), the subject is susceptible to disease.[30] Disease means precisely being in opposition to the totality, opposing placement within it:

> The subject therefore finds itself involved in a contradiction between the totality systematized in its consciousness and the particular determinateness that is not fluidified and given its place and rank within it. This is madness [*Verrücktheit*]. [*Enz.* § 408]

In madness it is as though one made the futile attempt to remain outside a whole whose very nature is to have no outside. It is as though one sought vainly to lose oneself beyond all hope of recovery, as though one sought to exceed a totality whose very nature is such as to prohibit in the end all excess.

Hegel actually describes certain forms of imagination as madness. For example, madness is said to supervene upon a person when he "believes his simply subjective presentation to be objectively present and clings to it in spite of the actual objectivity by which it is contradicted." Such persons might, Hegel adds, "imagine that they are someone *else*" (*Enz.* § 408 *Zusatz*). Hegel mentions also several cases of imagined illnesses. Here especially his strategy becomes transparent. Either the madman's position outside the whole is to be declared a matter of incurable disease, madness thus being isolated from reason and hence disarmed; or else, his position is to be reassimilated dialectically to that whole that it would then prove not to have exceeded. Of this second possibility Hegel writes as follows:

> In the case of an imagined illness, for example, it is often the case that the madman can be cured by appearing to adopt the person's distorted view, and then suddenly doing something that gives him a glimpse of what it is to be free of the malady.

He illustrates this dialectical therapy with the following example:

> Another person, who considered himself to be dead, remained motionless, and refused to eat, recovered his understanding in

the following manner. Someone else, pretending to share in his folly, placed him in a coffin, and took him to a vault where there was another person, also in a coffin, who pretended at first to be dead. After the fool had been there for a while, however, the other person sat up and said how pleased he was to have company in death. Then he got up and ate the food he had by him, telling the astonished newcomer that he had been dead for some time and therefore knew how the dead went about things. The fool was taken in by this assurance, followed suit by eating and drinking, and was cured. [*Enz.* § 408 *Zusatz*]

Even the most extreme possible attempt in imagination to lose oneself—imagining that one is dead—can be dialectically reversed into a recovery of self, a resurrection; or else, it can, granted the displacement, be declared incurable disease.

Let me return to Hegel's psychological presentation of imagination in order now to let the question multiply. It is a question of the subordination of imagination to presentation—to presentation in all three senses but preeminently in that sense appropriate to spirit as such, presentation as the self-presentation of spirit, as absolute self-presentation. In its inception imagination takes over the stock of images issuing forth from the nocturnal pit, brings them forth voluntarily without the aid even of those corresponding intuitions that were still required for recollection. Here it is a matter of "dissolving [*zerteilen*] the noctural gloom enveloping its wealth of images and banishing [*verscheuchen*] it by means of the bright clarity of presence [*durch die lichtvolle Klarheit der Gegenwärtigkeit*]" (*Enz.* § 455 *Zusatz*). The question is whether the nocturnal pit can be so thoroughly illuminated by the light of presence or whether even after the advent of reproductive imagination there do not remain withdrawn in its dark depths slumbering images that are not simply at the call of spirit. And does the noctural pit perhaps cast its shadow over the entire course of imagination? Do even those images brought forth from the pit by reproductive imagination not bring along something of its darkness, mixing it then into that play of images from which spirit would draw up universality? Is there in that play of images a dark residue, something not recoverable in universality, something resistant to that subjugating of images that would make them in the end only the mirror for spirit? Can one pass over that transition over which Hegel himself appears to have labored, the shift in the content of the universality operative in phantasy? What about this shift from a universality that would merely constitute the connection between the particulars belonging to the stock of images *to* a universality that would derive its very content from intelligence itself rather than from the stock of images from which it was first raised? What about this shift that allows intelligence then to subjugate the stock of images and to find in it only a mirror of itself? What about the shift "with which," as the Hotho transcription expresses it, "the realm of presentation is closed"?[31] Is there a residue that it merely represses rather than sublating? Or, differently regarded, is there a residue that is absolutely lost beyond all hope of recovery? And would such a residue be, with still more finality, left behind, assimilated, in the transition from symbol to sign? Or might even the sign be drawn back toward the pit from which it would have emerged, drawn back to the symbol as its metaphorical supplement—as, for example, when the sign itself comes in Hegel's own sober text to be called a pyramid?

Near the threshold of Hegel's presentation of presentation there is a discussion (*Enz.* § 449 *Zusatz*) in which reference is made to Aristotle, to his saying that all knowledge has its beginning in *wonder*. A Hegelian interpretation of that saying is then offered: at the beginning there is tension between the irrationality with which the object is burdened and the merely indeterminate certainty that spirit has of finding itself in that object; and it is precisely because of this tension that one is at the beginning inspired with wonder. But then the self-presentation of spirit is to resolve that particular tension and thus "philosophical thought has to raise itself above the standpoint of wonder." The question is whether on the way from pit to pyramid, the way of imagination, there is not an excess, a darkness that is irreducible to mere irrationality, that cannot be merely coaxed back to the life of spirit, like the madman who imagined that he was dead. Such excessive imagination, such phantasy drawn back toward the pit, toward a withdrawal from presence, could perhaps broach a wonder that one could never aspire to surpass.

NOTES

OCCLUSION

1. Friedrich Nietzsche, *Werke: Kritische Gesamtausgabe*, ed. G. Colli and M. Montinari (Berlin: Walter de Gruyter, 1969), VI 3:69.

2. Ibid., 75.

3. "To invent fables [*zu fabeln*] about a world 'other' than this one has no sense at all, unless an instinct of slander, detraction, and suspicion against life is powerful in us: in this case we avenge ourselves against life with the phantasmagoria of 'another,' a 'better' life" (ibid., 72). Note also in this passage the reference to phantasy, i.e., to imagination.

4. In his discussion of "the error of imaginary causes [*Irrthum der imaginären Ursachen*]" Nietzsche tells of how in dreams a kind of "apparent reversal of time" can occur by which what is really later comes to be regarded as cause; he concludes: "The representations that a certain state has *produced* have been misunderstood as its causes." He adds: "In fact, we do the same thing when awake" (ibid., 86).

5. Ibid., 72.

6. "How the 'True World' Finally Became a Fable" (ibid., 74–75).

7. Compare Plato, *Phaedrus* 248b, and *Republic* 621a.

CHAPTER ONE

1. Plato, *Phaedo* 96e–99e.

2. Immanuel Kant, *Kritik der reinen Vernunft*, ed. Raymund Schmidt (Hamburg: Felix Meiner Verlag, 1956), A 852/B 880–A 856/B 884; citations are given according to the pagination of the first (A) and second (B) editions, as presented in Schmidt's text, and will be included parenthetically in the text. References to Kant's other writings will be by volume and page number of *Kants*

Gesammelte Schriften, ed. Preussische Akademie der Wissenschaft (Berlin, 1902–), and will also be given parenthetically in the text.

CHAPTER TWO

1. References to Fichte's works are to volume number and page number of *Fichtes Werke*, ed. I. H. Fichte (Berlin: Walter de Gruyter, 1971), which is a reprint of the editions of 1845–46 and 1834–35. References will be given in parentheses in the text. Use has also been made of the critical edition being issued by the Bayerische Akademie der Wissenschaften: J. G. Fichte, *Gesamtausgabe*, ed. R. Lauth and H. Jacob (Stuttgard–Bad Cannstatt: Friedrich Frommann Verlag, 1964–).

2. In the *Second Introduction to the Wissenschaftslehre* (1798) Fichte, reaffirming his solidarity with Kantianism, notes how extensively this solidarity is contested: "All who rank as well-acquainted with the Kantian philosophy and have given their opinion on the matter—both friends and foes of the *Wissenschaftslehre*—are unanimous in affirming the contrary, and *at their urging* the same has been said by Kant himself, who, after all, must undoubtedly understand himself the best" (1:469). Fichte adds in a note: "I, for my part, have so far found it impossible to learn, on the best or on any authority, the Kantian opinion of the *Wissenschaftslehre*. . . ." The following year Kant was challenged by a reviewer in the *Erlanger Literaturzeitung*, who asked whether his theories were to be taken literally or as interpreted by Fichte or Beck. Kant—apparently without having read the *Wissenschaftslehre*, relying instead on his disciple Johann Schultz for an account of Fichte's position—publicly dissociated himself from Fichte in his open letter on Fichte's *Wissenschaftslehre* (*Kants Gesammelte Schriften*, 12:370–71, 7 August 1799): ". . . I hereby declare that I regard Fichte's *Wissenschaftslehre* as a totally indefensible system. For the pure theory of science is nothing more or less than mere logic, and the principles of logic cannot lead to any material knowledge. . . . and so it is enough that I renounce any connection with that philosophy. . . . There is an Italian proverb: May God protect us from our friends, and we shall watch out for our enemies ourselves." Fichte's response in an open letter to Schelling was restrained. Kant's objection that the *Wissenschaftslehre* is merely logic is, Fichte explains, merely a semantic dispute beneath which, he insists, there remains fundamental agreement. He continues:

"It is only to be expected, dear Schelling, that just as the defenders of the pre-Kantian metaphysics have not yet ceased telling Kant that he is occupying himself with fruitless subtleties, Kant should say the same to us. It is only to be expected that, just as they assert against Kant that their metaphysics still stands undamaged, unimprovable, and unalterable in all eternity, Kant should assert the same about his against us. Who knows where even now the young fiery head may be at work who will go beyond the principles of the *Wissenschaftslehre* and try to prove its errors and incompleteness" (Johann Gottlieb Fichte and Friedrich Wilhelm Joseph von Schelling, *Briefwechsel* [Frankfurt am Main: Suhrkamp, 1968], 65–67).

3. The order of the I, the you, the one(self), is thematized in that "history of language projected a priori" in Fichte's text "Von der Sprachfähigkeit und dem Ursprunge der Sprache." According to this account, all speech originally occurred in the third person, for one called the other person by his proper name: *N. N. soll das thun!* Note what serves to establish the third person as (a priori) historically first: that the entire ordering is preceded by the operation of proper names. Agreements and contracts prompt the transition to second person, for one then feels the need of saying to the other: *das sollst "Du" thun.* The first person, *das "Ich,"* comes last, for it attests to a higher *Vernunftkultur: "Ich* drückt den höchsten Charakter der Vernunft aus" (8:334–35). The Fichtean text, at least every initiatory text, would retrace this order, would repeat this history of the turn from things to oneself as a you and then as I.

4. The fact that the text does not deal with the spirit and the letter in philosophy was pointed out by its reviewers, e.g., in the *Neue allgemeine deutsche Bibliothek*: "The inner voice of the artist is the spirit of his product; and the accidental forms in which he expresses it are the body or letter thereof. Quite correct! We do not yet learn what the spirit of a philosphy would be; the continuation that is promised will probably make it known." This incompleteness was one of the major criticisms offered by Schiller when he sent the manuscript back to Fichte rather than publishing it as planned in *Die Horen.* Though Schiller's letter is lost, one of the drafts for it reads as follows: you "deal with nothing but spirit in the fine arts, which as far as I know is something quite different from the opposite of the letter. . . . Still less do I comprehend how you will find a way from spirit in Goethe's work . . . to spirit in the Kantian or Leibnizian philosophy." In his letter responding to the return of his manuscript Fichte insisted on the affinity of art and philosophy:

"Spirit in philosophy and spirit in fine art are just as closely akin as are all species of the same genus." Though in his response Fichte stated that he would finish the text and then send it to Schiller again, the continuation beyond the third letter never appeared. Regarding the history of the text and the exchange with Schiller, see *Gesamtausgabe*, I 6:315–32.

5. The complex structure of the systematic reflections, both the reflection by way of conceptual determination and the ensuing, more properly enactmental reflection, is outlined by Fichte in the *Grundlage der gesammten Wissenschaftslehre* (1:219ff.). The determination of properly philosophical thought as a double enactment by which the *Sache* would be brought to show itself from itself to the contemplative philosopher—this determination is of course taken over, though also contested and transformed, in Schelling's *System des transcendentalen Idealismus* and in Hegel's *Phänomenologie des Geistes* and is vigorously renewed in twentieth-century phenomenology.

6. Fichte stresses no less than Kant the constitutive value of completeness for the system of human knowledge or of reason (in the broadest sense)—e.g., in the following marginal note: "Thus the *Wissenschaftslehre* has absolute totality. In it one leads to all, and all to one. However, it is the only science that can be completed; completion is accordingly its distinguishing characteristic. All other sciences are infinite and can never be completed; for they do not proceed back into their fundamental principle" (1:59n.). The circling back to the fundamental principle thus constitutes the *Wissenschaftslehre* as finite or limited and distinguishes it as such from all other sciences.

7. "For in reason there is present no deception at all" (1:514).

8. "It is impossible to reflect without having abstracted" (1:72).

9. For the few formulations that I borrow here from the *Introductions* the question of their retrospective character is relatively inconsequential. But clearly they do differ in certain respects from the *Grundlage der gesammten Wissenschaftslehre* of 1794, e.g., in the use of the expression "intellectual intuition" (*intellectuelle Anschauung*); the question, which I leave open here, is whether these differences bespeak some "development" that would set the point of view of the *Introductions* decisively apart from that of the texts of 1794–95.

10. Fichte calls attention to the procedural circle that is in force

here, namely, that the laws of ordinary logic are presupposed and can only later be actually derived from those fundamental principles to which at the outset they lead. Fichte grants: "This is a circle; but it is an unavoidable circle," and he refers explicitly to the discussion of this kind of circularity in "Ueber den Begiff der Wissenschaftslehre" (1:92). In each case, once he arrives at the fundamental principle, Fichte proceeds to derive the corresponding logical law from it (cf. 1:99, 105).

11. It must be insisted that these and other such terms be understood in the precise senses determined (or redetermined) for them in the *Kritik der reinen Vernunft* and the *Grundlage der gesammten Wissenschaftslehre* and that recent connotations be kept out of action. For example, *reality (Realität)* belongs to the category of quality; it does not mean *existence (Dasein)* or *actuality (Wirklichkeit)* but rather designates the totality of elements ("reals") that constitute *what* something is.

CHAPTER THREE

1. A measure of this richness and complexity is provided by the range of meanings and the extent of etymological connections that are given for the relevant words in the *Oxford English Dictionary*. Only a few of these have been excerpted here.

2. One could refer to such textual spacing in order to characterize with a certain structural precision the Heideggerian reading of Kant's text in *Kant und das Problem der Metaphysik* (1929; 4th ed., Frankfurt am Main: Vittorio Klostermann, 1973). What then appears distinctive about Heidegger's reading is its marginal character. In contrast to a reading that would confine itself to the text of the *Critique of Pure Reason*, recasting that text in an allegedly equivalent but more transparent form, perhaps, in addition, criticizing that text from some position outside it—in contrast to such a reading, Heidegger's links up with the margin of that text, holds in focus certain prearticulating traces that lie outside yet frame the text. More precisely, Heidegger's reading takes up that margin in its engagement with the text—that is, his reading in effect resumes the movement between margin and text, specifically, the movement in which certain developments in the text recoil upon the framing margin, deforming the frame, filling the margin. And yet, in resuming the movement, Heidegger's reading also transforms it. The movement as resumed within the reading is no longer merely the interplay between margin and text, no longer merely

something happening on the end of the Kantian text. Rather, Heidegger's reading shifts the edge to the center—that is, it converts the interplay between margin and text into an essentially textual movement, a textual movement that, implicit in Kant, would be made explicit in the Heideggerian resumption. The frame of prearticulating traces becomes part of the picture itself. What was outside the Kantian text becomes part of a positive thematic. It is because such transformation governs the Heideggerian reading that a tacit identification can be made between two different ways of characterizing that reading (cf. Heidegger, *Kant und das Problem der Metaphysik*, 195–96). On the one hand, the reading is to expose the unsaid (*das Ungesagte*) that can be gleaned through what is said (*das Gesagte*). On the other hand, the reading is "to make manifest what Kant brought to light . . . above and beyond his express formulations"; it is to make explicit what he wanted to say but did not succeed in saying. It would be possible to distinguish another kind of reading that, while remaining marginal, would forgo making this identification, would forgo assuming that the unsaid is something that belongs, even if only implicitly, to the Kantian thematic—that is, would forgo assuming that the unsaid is something virtually intended within the thematic field but not brought to expression, something that Kant would have said had he been able to render sufficiently transparent the complex fundamental intention constituted in and through the deed of critique. It would be a matter of opening the possibility that the unsaid, Kant's silence, might fall entirely outside the domain of this simple opposition between what he said and what he only virtually intended—that is, the possibility that it might fall outside the thematic of the Kantian text, that it might lie in the margin of that text. The possibility of such a marginal unsaid would broach, then, the possibility of a reading that would preserve the margin as such instead of transforming the play of margin and text into a new text; such a style of reading, which is very sketchily exemplified below, would preserve the prearticulative character of the marginal traces and, leaving them outside the text, would follow the lines of movement marked on the edge of the Kantian text.

3. Compare John Sallis, *The Gathering of Reason* (Athens: Ohio University Press, 1980), 21–25.

CHAPTER FOUR

1. *Kants Gesammelte Schriften*, 2:209–10.

2. I. Kant, *Kritik der Urteilskraft*, Vorrede. Further references to this work are given in parentheses in the text. References to the work proper are by section number; references to the Vorrede or the Einleitung are designated by "V" or "E," respectively.

3. The word *sie* is ambiguous here and could refer to *Auffassung*, to *Formen*, to *Einbildungskraft*, or of course to any combination of these.

4. Erste Fassung der Einleitung in die *Kritik der Urteilskraft*, VIII.

5. Kant characterizes the feeling not only as a feeling of the harmony of the free play but also as a feeling of the *freedom* in the free play. Thus: "On this feeling of freedom in the play of our cognitive faculties, which must at the same time be purposive . . ." (§ 45). Only if the intentional or disclosive character of the feeling involved in the judgment of taste is suppressed does it become necessary to invoke a special act of empirical judgment that would confirm the connection between the harmonious free play and the feeling (of pleasure), the latter being considered then as simply due to, i.e., grounded on, the former. This is a principal point on which the interpretation here merely outlined would, if developed, diverge from such interpretations as that given by Paul Guyer in *Kant and the Claims of Taste* (Cambridge, Mass.: Harvard University Press, 1979), esp. 8, 68, 99–110.

6. Compare Gilles Deleuze, *Kant's Critical Philosophy: The Doctrine of the Faculties*, trans. H. Tomlinson and B. Habberjam (Minneapolis: University of Minnesota Press, 1984), 58–61.

7. The relation is much less simply a matter of difference if knowledge is taken in its a priori synthetic determination, or, more precisely, if one considers that a priori operation by which objects are first constituted as such, an operation that Kant continues— despite considerable displacement—to regard as a kind of cognition.

8. Rudolf Makkreel has drawn attention to this important point, which is especially obscured by the Bernard translation of the *Critique of Judgment*: "The idea of form might be thought inappropriate in the context of the sublime, for it is widely interpreted to be formless. However, Kant does not write that the

sublime can be found *only* in a formless object, but that it can *also* be found there. In an earlier quote Kant indicated that the sublime involves a purposiveness of the subject 'in respect of objects according to their form or even their formlessness . . .' [E VII]. Thus what is judged to be sublime is not necessarily formless" (Rudolf Makkreel, "Imagination and Temporality in Kant's Theory of the Sublime," *Journal of Aesthetics and Art Criticism* 42, no. 3 [Spring 1984]:313).

9. In the precritical work *Observations on the Feeling of the Beautiful and Sublime* (1764) Kant offers the following examples of the sublime: "The sight of a mountain whose snow-covered peak rises above the clouds, the description of a raging storm, or Milton's portrayal of the infernal kingdom." These are contrasted with the following examples of the beautiful: "The sight of a meadow filled with flowers, valleys with windings brooks and covered with grazing flocks, the description of Elysium, or Homer's portrayal of the girdle of Venus." The division into the mathematically sublime and the dynamically sublime is missing. Instead there is a threefold division into (1) the terrifying sublime (*das Schreckhaft-erhabene*), in which the feeling of sublime is accompanied by a certain dread or melancholy, (2) the noble (*das Edle*), in which that feeling is accompanied merely by quiet wonder, and (3) the splendid (*das Prächtige*), in which it is accompanied by a beauty completely pervading a sublime plan. For the second and third types, respectively, Kant cites two examples that are retained and, as will be seen below, figure quite prominently in the *Critique of Judgment*, that of a pyramid and of St. Peter's in Rome. (*Beobachtungen über das Gefühl des Schönen und Erhabenen*, in *Kants Gesammelte Schriften*, 2:208–10.)

10. Compare *Anthropologie in pragmatischer Hinsicht*, in *Kants Gesammelte Schriften*, 7:153. In the *Critique of Judgment* (§ 27), this identification is explicitly made.

11. There is another passage too that openly refers to the character of the reflection as schematism: "For the imagination by the laws of association makes our state of contentment physically dependent; but it also, by the principles of the schematism of judgment (thus to that exent subordinated to freedom), is the instrument of reason and its ideas and as such is a power of maintaining our independence of natural influences . . ." (§ 29).

12. On the one hand, the moral law in determining the will thwarts the subject's inclination, checking selfishness and striking

down self-conceit; but in this very process the moral law becomes also an object of positive respect, engenders in the moral subject a feeling for the law. Let the following two passages suffice to mark this issue, this point from which an investigation of the interconnection between the *Critique of Practical Reason* and the *Critique of Judgment* would need primarily to proceed. (1) "If anything checks our self-conceit in our own judgment, it humiliates. Therefore, the moral law inevitably humbles every man when he compares the sensible propensity of his nature with the law. Now if the idea of something as the determining ground of the will humiliates us in our self-consciousness, it awakens respect for itself so far as it is positive and the ground of determination. The moral law, therefore, is even subjectively a cause of respect" (*Kants Gesammelte Schriften*, 5:74). (2) "The lowering of the pretentions of moral self-esteem (humiliation) on the sensible side is an elevation of the moral, i.e., practical esteem for the law on the intellectual side" (ibid., 79).

13. Most notably the following passage, which has been cited above in part: "But this movement ought to be judged as subjectively purposive (because the sublime pleases): thus it is referred by the imagination either to the faculty of cognition or to the faculty of desire" (§ 24).

14. "Therefore the feeling of the sublime in nature is respect for our own destination [*Achtung für unsere eigene Bestimmung*], which, by a certain subreption, we attribute to an object of nature . . ." (§ 27).

15. Compare Makkreel's discussion of the entire passage on the suspension of time and his explication of it by reference to certain passages in the *Critique of Pure Reason* ("Imagination and Temporality," esp. 305–9).

CHAPTER FIVE

1. The following discussion is limited almost exclusively to the philosophy of spirit as expressed in the third part of Hegel's *Encyclopedia of the Philosophical Sciences*, some account being taken of the differences between the three editions of this work (1817, 1827, 1830). In particular, it has not been possible to include within the present framework a discussion of the development of the philosophy of spirit during Hegel's Jena period. As regards the problem of imagination, Petry points to a certain continuity: "By 1805/6, he was already treating imagination in a way which was

not so very different from that of the mature Encyclopedia" (M. J. Petry, ed., *Hegel's Philosophy of Subjective Spirit* [Dordrecht: D. Reidel, 1978], 3:408). But clearly this development needs to be thoroughly investigated now that the texts of the Jena period have been issued by the Hegel-Archiv. For the following discussion I have used primarily Petry's edition, which contains a photographic reproduction of the third edition published by Hegel in 1830 as well as the *Zusätze* added by Boumann when he republished this material in 1845. Petry's edition also indicates variations between the third and the second (1827) edition. I have also consulted the text prepared by Nicolin and Pöggeler (*Enzyklopädie der philosophischen Wissenschaften im Grundrisse (1830)*, ed. F. Nocolin and O. Pöggeler [Hamburg: Felix Meiner, 1959]). For the first edition (1817) I have used a copy in the possession of the Hegel-Archiv in Bochum. The designation *Enz.* followed by a section number refers to the third edition, unless otherwise indicated. References to *Zusätze* are identified as such.

2. Compare, e.g., Hegel's description of the *Phenomenology of Spirit* as "die Darstellung des erscheinenden Wissens" (*Phänomenologie des Geistes* [Hamburg: Felix Meiner, 1952], 66).

3. Fichte, *Werke*, 1:284.

4. "The spirit that, so developed, knows itself as spirit is *science*. Science is the actuality of spirit and the realm that spirit builds for itself in its own element" (Hegel, *Phänomenologie des Geistes*, 24).

5. Aristotle, *Metaphysics* 982b 11–14; *Enz.* § 449 (*Zusatz*).

6. Kehler MS, 56 (cited in Petry, ed., 1:11).

7. The quotations suggest that Hegel especially admired Aristotle's recognition of the soul's progression in degree of complexity. Compare Petry, ed., 1:145; and also G. W. F. Hegel, *Vorlesungen über die Geschichte der Philosophie* (Frankfurt am Main: Suhrkamp, 1971), 2:203.

8. As Hicks observes, one would have expected Aristotle to use διάνοια (instead of ὑπόληψις) in the second clause as he did in the first. Hicks proposes the following connection: "Thus διάνοια is the process of which ὑπόληψις is the result." (Aristotle, *De Anima*, ed. R. D. Hicks [Cambridge, 1907], 457.)

9. Aristotle explicitly excludes here "what we say metaphorically" about φαντασία. According to Hicks, the wider, metaphorical sense is based on the felt connection of φαντασία with φαίνεσθαι. In this wider sense "φαντασία means presenta-

tion, appearance, and any of the cognitive faculties, or again even sense-perception, may be described as presentative; that is, the result they produce is something present to the soul, something that appears (ὁ φαίνεται)" (460–61). Hegel would no doubt have found very pertinent the way in which the Greek language thus identifies and yet distinguishes imagination and presentation.

10. This character is considered by Aristotle, not in the principal account of imagination (bk. 3, chap. 3), but in a supplementary account dealing more generally with the role of imagination in the origination of movement and of action. Specifically, the statement "ὥστε δύναται ἓν ἐκ πλειόνων φαντασμάτων ποιεῖν" (434 a 10) occurs within the framework of a distinction introduced in that context between sensible imagination (αἰσθητικὴ φαντασία) and deliberative imagination (βουλευτικὴ φαντασία). The power of combining many images into one is explicitly ascribed only to the latter. Compare the discussion in D. A. Rees, "Aristotle's Treatment of Φαντασία," *Essays in Ancient Greek Philosophy*, ed. John P. Anton and George L. Kustas (Albany: State University of New York Press, 1971), 1:500–501.

11. This formulation (428 a 1–2) is repeated in a somewhat different form in *On Dreams*, 459 a 18.

12. Compare Hicks, 467–68.

13. Ibid., 459.

14. Compare *Poetics* 1448 b 2–3.

15. In his lecture notes on the corresponding section of the 1817 edition, Hegel writes: "Der Intelligenz ist Inhalt gegeben, macht ihn zu dem ihrigen. *producirt denselben in sich.* Assimilation" ("Hegels Vorlesungsnotizen zum subjektiven Geist," ed. F. Nicolin and H. Schneider, *Hegel-Studien* 10 [1975]: 53).

16. On the other hand, practical spirit or will proceeds in the opposite direction, beginning with its own aims and interests and proceeding to make these objective. Free spirit unites theoretical and practical, eliminating the one-sidedness of each.

17. Hegel's use of the title "psychology" (which did not appear until the 1827 ed.) could be taken to suggest that what Aristotle treats in his work "Περὶ Ψυχῆς" is the same as that which Hegel treats under the rubric "spirit." But this cannot be entirely or simply the case in view, e.g., of Hegel's statement that the soul as dealt with in his anthropology is "the passive νοῦς of Aristotle" (*Enz.* § 389). Without proposing any detailed correspondence between Aristotle's treatise and all or part of Hegel's philosophy of

subjective spirit, it suffices to observe that spirit (as the subject of psychology) is the *truth* of soul, suffices for establishing that in conceiving imagination as a *faculty of spirit* Hegel is thinking through to the end the Aristotelian determination of imagination as a *faculty of the soul*. Hegel's placing of imagination on the side of *theoretical* spirit would also appear to be prepared by the Aristotelian analysis, which, distinguishing practical thinking (φρονεῖν) from intelligence (νοεῖν), then places imagination in relation to powers associated with νοεῖν. One difficult passage even suggests that φαντασία is a kind of νοεῖν, along with ὑπόληψις (cf. 427 b).

18. Hegel, *Vorlesungen über die Geschichte der Philosophie*, 2:199. In the first edition of the *Encyclopedia* (1817) Hegel points out that, "as regards faculty, the *dynamis* of Aristotle has an entirely different meaning" (§ 368)—i.e., Aristotle understood faculty (δύναμις) in a way entirely different from those who take a faculty to be a fixed, isolated determinateness.

19. It is important to bear in mind that *Erinnerung* has for Hegel not only the sense of remembrance but also of inwardizing or collecting into oneself. In fact, in its first two moments it has almost exclusively the latter sense, coming to have the sense of remembrance only in its third moment. *Recollection* has the advantage of preserving both senses and also, not inappropriately, of alluding to ἀνάμνησις.

20. Boumann's foreward to his edition is reprinted in Petry, ed., 1:cl–lvii.

21. *Hervorrufen* in the first edition (1817).

22. In § 454: "Intelligence is therefore the power of being able to express [*äussern*] what it possesses, and of no longer requiring external intuition in order to have this possession existing within itself." This is also confirmed in Hegel's lecture notes: "Reprod[ucirende Intelligenz] bedarf der Empf[indung] Unm[ittelbarkeit] der Ansch[auung] n[icht] mehr" (Nicolin and Schneider, eds., "Hegels Vorlesungsnotizen," 62).

23. To grasp association in this way is already to surpass association as commonly understood in discussions of so-called association of ideas. In Griesheim's unpublished transcription of Hegel's 1825 lectures on subjective spirit, a detailed contrast is drawn between mere association and a determining that brings into play the distinction between universal and particular, i.e., that produces the universal presentation by way of abstraction (Staats-

bibliothek Preussischer Kulturbesitz, Berlin, Griesheim MS, 394–95).

24. The corresponding passage in the 1830 edition reads: "In itself, however, intelligence is not only a general form, for its inwardness is internally determined concrete subjectivity, with a capacity of its own deriving, insofar as such a content can be spoken of in anticipation, from some interest, implicit concept, or idea." In Hotho's unpublished transcription of Hegel's 1822 lectures on subjective spirit, a more specific indication is given: "Die allg[emeine] Vorstellung . . . kann ihrem fernen [?] Inhalt nach entstehen, diß geht uns hier nichts an. Sie kann im innern, im Sittlichen ihren Quell haben" (Staatsbibliothek Preussischer Kulturbesitz, Berlin, Hotho MS, 91).

25. Nicolin and Schneider, eds., "Hegels Vorlesungnotizen," 62.

26. Petry, ed., 1:cliii.

27. Hans-Christian Lucas, who is on the staff of the Hegel-Archiv in Bochum and is working with these texts, has communicated that, as far as he knows, the Griesheim transcription is the only one of the sources for Boumann's *Zusätze* that is still available today.

28. Hotho MS, 91. Compare Griesheim MS, 346–49.

29. At the end of § 457 proper, at precisely the point where he introduces that form, he characterizes intelligence thus determined as *producirend*.

30. It is not without significance that in the *Philosophical Propadeutic* (1808ff.) these forms are not displaced but treated under the heading "Imagination" and along with the other forms such as reproductive and productive imagination (cf. Georg Wilhelm Friedrich Hegel, *Werke in zwanzig Bänden* [Frankfurt am Main: Suhrkamp, 1970], 4:46ff).

31. "Hiemit ist da Reich d[er] Vorstellung geschlossen" (Hotho MS, 91).

INDEX